BALANCHINE

Celebrating a Life in Dance

PHOTOGRAPHS BY COSTAS

EDITED BY COSTAS

TIDE-MARK PRESS

WINDSOR, CONNECTICUT

Copyright © 2003 Costas
Published by Tide-mark Press, Ltd.
P.O. Box 20, Windsor, Connecticut 06095-0020

Printed in Korea by Samhwa Printing Co.

Copyeditors: Barbara Palfy and Edwin Bacher
Page Design: Dan Veale

Library of Congress Cataloging-in-Publication Data
Costas
Balanchine: Celebrating a Life in Dance
256 p. cm.
Includes Index

ISBN 1-55949-845-5 Hardcover

Library of Congress Control Number
2003106324

Contents

Introduction

On January 22, 2004, people around the world will be celebrating—in various ways—the 100th anniversary of Balanchine's birth. This book toasts that event.

The great American dance critic Edwin Denby said (and I'm paraphrasing this), that he wanted to thank Mr. Balanchine for helping him to see ballet. Those of us who were lucky enough to serve Mr. B did indeed learn to see ballet anew, and learned other things as well.

One day, Mr. B, waiting for an elevator in the New York State Theater, started talking to me. Wanting to hear the rest of what he was saying, I followed him upstairs and into the big studio on the fifth floor, where he proceeded to choreograph a new pas de deux for his *Don Quixote*. This ballet was scheduled to be danced for a week and never to be seen again. I did not understand his need to spend time and effort on a work that would not be seen in the future.

Many years later I was working on a book on Greek myths. While in Delphi, Greece, I marveled at the famous statue of the charioteer. In ancient times it stood in a chariot, so positioned that the feet could not be seen by anyone—except by the gods, of course. Yet the sculptor had perfected the tendons of the charioteer's feet as diligently as the visible portions of the body. It was then that I remembered and finally understood *the Don Quixote* incident.

Mr. Balanchine was an accomplished musician. On occasion, he composed and even wrote piano reductions of orchestral scores. His love and respect for music were enormous. In programs, he listed the composer before the choreographer—a practice that is still in use today at New York City Ballet and almost nowhere else.

My first inclination was to classify the ballets according to their music. When friends whose judgement I trust pointed out the shortcomings of my effort, I challenged them to find a better system of classification only to find that their suggestions had shortcomings as well. What to do about this, I wondered. A few weeks later, the story of Alexander the Great and the Gordian knot came to mind. Why not cut to the core of the problem and just list them alphabetically? So that's how you will find them on the following pages.

There are many people I want to thank. First and foremost, Mr. Balanchine, for allowing me to enter his magical kingdom and giving me access to rehearsals and choreographic sessions, among other things; Lincoln Kirstein, who insisted that I be able to photograph the company on a regular basis; Barbara Horgan, who made this book possible; Karin von Aroldingen, for championing my photos and bringing them to the attention of Mr. Balanchine; Nancy Reynolds, for using my work over so many years; Marvin Hoshino, for his enormous technical help with this book and with my photos in general; and George Jackson, who gave me my first Leica and saw to it that I got to know a lot of Balanchine's ballets early on. I also want to thank Peter Martins, Virginia Donaldson and all her successors at the Press Office, Lorie Barber, Debbie Koolish, Richard Dryden, Tom Kelley, Jacqueline Mooney, Mari Eckroate, George Maas, Joseph Goldin, John Healy, all the writers of this book, Scott Kaeser and Jennifer Renk at Tide-mark Press, and finally you, who have chosen to read this book.

—Costas

The Kirov Ballet in Symphony in C

The Art of Balanchine

by George Jackson

Golden are the days in which advances of technique go hand-in-hand with the evolution of new work. Once upon a time in ballet there was a long spell of such days. That was when George Balanchine served as both teacher and choreographer for one and the same institution, the New York City Ballet. His two endeavors resonated, resulting in dancing and choreography that amplified each other. The Balanchine dancer became part of the Balanchine ballet, and one could tell them apart only when a cast not trained by him performed that repertory.

Balanchine was no stranger to teaching, not just in rehearsal as every choreographer must, but also in class. However, he did not teach consistently during his earlier career. It was in preparation for the New York City Ballet's first visit overseas, to London in 1950, that he began teaching regularly and for all ranks of the company. Thereafter, Balanchine continued to give company class frequently into 1982, the year before he died.

At least nine characteristics distinguish the Balanchine dancer. Typically, there is an about-to-be-in-motion readiness, even at rest. Preferably, the body is streamlined and long in the legs. The spine is highly pulled up. Placement is slightly angular, which imparts to surrounding space a cubist inflection. In motion, there is a tendency to speed. Phrasing is syncopated, making one think, in passing, of jazz. The movement's pronounced emphasis is from the waist down. Moreover, continuity of the dance impulse is critical, and yet the flow is not necessarily

Jerome Robbins, Lincoln Kirstein, Peter Martins, Mikhail Baryshnikov and members of New York City Ballet during The Balanchine Celebration, May 4 – June 27, 1993

Nilas Martins in Orpheus

lyrical. And, when one looked in those days, all these things appeared more distinctly in the female dancer than in the male. Nevertheless, Balanchine did choreography for circus elephants, too ("… / Mr. B, though / never did go / on safari. / If he had gone, / he would have known / elephants are / [Martha] Graham dancers/ and wanted, instead, / the agile giraffe"). One can only wonder what Balanchine would have made for the Lipizzaner stallions if his

patron and sparring partner, Lincoln Kirstein, had succeeded in establishing a Spanish Riding School at Saratoga.

There is no nine-point checklist for Balanchine's ballets. The pieces he choreographed are too diverse, although his handiwork is apparent in all of them. Balanchine worked simultaneously on multiple levels. Consider the finale of his Bizet *Symphony in C.* It is,

as spectacle, a ballabile that knocks you over with its form, force, and logic. The distinct motifs of the ballet's preceding sections, and the very dancers who had stated them, appear again not only for recapitulation's sake but in order to dance together in summation of the symphony. Beyond itself, this danced defile refracts centuries of theatrical endings, becoming an apotheosis of the classical tradition and, perhaps, a model of social order. There is entertainment value, formal beauty, process made tangible, awe, and meaning in these few minutes that seem like a whirlwind suspension of time.

For *The Prodigal Son,* Balanchine chose a step from a fool's dance of Siberian origin—a side-to-side pendulation in squatting position with the legs wide open and the knees bent—as the characteristic motion of the strangers who prey on the hero. The step is silly, giddy, and unballetic, but Balanchine stylized it somewhat (squatting almost becomes a plié, the open legs approximate second position and, at times, the raised arms mirror the lower limbs). This transformation results in a more weighted appearance that suits the story, for the strangers

look grotesque and alien. Yet the original image of the fool, the clown, is not erased. Rather, it enriches the repulsive, frightening new aspect. This ability to adopt movement into the ballet tradition (in this instance, into the balletic character tradition) and make it seem coherent is as characteristic of Balanchine's work as the rich variety of his classical step vocabulary.

Balanchine rehearsed his Ravel *Rapsodie Espagnole* at a time when Mikhail Baryshnikov, having recently defected from the USSR, astonished American audiences with his ability to change direction in midair without visible preparation. Apparently, this facility of Baryshnikov's intrigued Balanchine too. It

fit in well with his striving for movement continuity. At the time, Balanchine had on hand another dancer he thought capable of mastering the technique and he incorporated demands for such perpetuum mobile into Peter Schaufuss's role for the Ravel ballet. To have seen the two, Balanchine and Schaufuss, still working after the premiere to make the movement even more like quicksilver cannot be forgotten by anyone lucky enough to have been a rehearsal witness that hot summer of 1975. Balanchine believed in the evolution of ballet. Earlier, in the 1950s, when films of virtuosic Soviet partnering—the throws and catches of Vassily Vainonen's *Moszkowski Waltz* and Asaf Messerer's *Spring Waters*—were first shown in the USA, he, too, had tried those things, rehearsing Tanaquil Le Clercq, Nicholas Magallanes, and Francisco Moncion in a pas de trois for the Triumphal Scene in New York City Opera's 1953 production of *Aida* at Chicago's Civic Opera House. Balanchine was always pushing the boundaries, whether from his own bountiful imagination or from things borrowed. ("Steal from the best," was his advice to young choreographers.)

There are many stories of how Balanchine worked in rehearsal. When he was trying to finish his Adagio Lamentoso for the Tchaikovsky *Symphony Pathétique,* a joint project with Jerome Robbins, time was running out. The premiere had been scheduled to occur and the audience was waiting in the New York State Theater's downstairs lobby. Balanchine threw up his hands and told the house manager to bring down the curtain and open the doors. What happened in the brief time span between the end of the rehearsal and the performance? Did Balanchine simply give his dancers verbal instructions? Whatever it was, what the audience was shown looked complete. The piece emerged as a memorial not just to Tchaikovsky, but also to the recently deceased Léonide Massine and his symphonic ballets, which were mystic Wagnerian liturgies of the sort Balanchine and his musical mentor,

Mr. Balanchine with Jacques d'Amboise and Rosemary Dunleavy on the set for Noah and the Ark

Suzanne Farrell and Peter Martins in Agon

instances when Balanchine changed steps because he no longer liked them or did not have a dancer able to do them justice. Whether Balanchine was working anew or doing rework, the results were clear. There was transparency whether the musicality was simple (Drigo, Minkus) or complex (Stravinsky, Schoenberg, et al.). The Verdi *Ballo della Regina,* for example, is a divertissement. It is a display of virtuosity in order to exhilarate the viewers and challenge the performers. Technical display culminates in the ballerina role. Mystery, though, resides in the principal male's part. He seems to be searching for a feminine ideal. This is clear, even if one does not know that the scenario for Verdi's music originally involved the quest for a perfect pearl. Other textures that surface

Mr. Balanchine with Jack Venza and Merrill Brockway on the set of Dance in America *for WNET*

Igor Stravinsky, found appropriate perhaps for houses of worship but not theaters. Conscious self-contradiction is another characteristic of geniuses.

When Balanchine worked apart from rehearsals, sitting at the piano and getting to know the score, he was very private. Music often determined the shape and the form of a Balanchine ballet as well as the choreography's weight, texture, counterpoint, and perfume. That did not preclude sensitivity to the other elements of theater. In *Firebird* and *Orpheus* he paid as close attention to Chagall's and Noguchi's decors, respectively, as to Stravinsky's music. He saw to it that movement and lighting complemented the stage pictures. In *Liebeslieder Walzer,* he appreciated the fun that Brahms had had in fitting his pianistic

waltzes to verses for the singers. And at the end, where Brahms had composed music to the words of a great poet, Goethe, the dancers simply sit and listen, lost in thought.

It is the way of the world and the fate of art that some of the meanings of an artwork are lost, even if the materials remain. Artists have used diverse strategies to try to avoid this sort of "becoming dated." Goethe recommended focusing on real topics—enduring nature rather than changeable society and transient convention. Sometimes Balanchine believed in embedding meaning into the steps. Yet, isn't our view of nature determined socially, by philosophy and science? Steps too, not just acting, can go flat, and there were many

A dancer from Les Ballets de Monte Carlo performs a scene from The Four Temperaments

in the music—the profound pressure of the sea depths and, from the surrounding opera story (*Don Carlos* after Schiller), the grandeur of Spanish court ritual—appear in the choreography. The viewer can make those associations or not. If not, there is nothing murky about those moments—they are simply modulations of virtuosity. In either case, or in between, the aim of Balanchine's ballets is the satisfaction they give the viewer and the invitation they extend to be seen again, because one suspects that further viewing will be very worthwhile.

Balanchine's influence has extended far beyond the realm of ballet. His idea of beauty "beyond Ginger Rogers" helped to shape the female body and women's fashions. As a craftsman who could choreograph in diverse ways—the classical, the

The Bolshoi Ballet in Symphony in C

contemporary, the surreal, and with or without a plot and characterization—he upset notions about period style in all the arts. Because his handiwork is recognizable no matter what the style, Balanchine remains inimitable. Happy 100th! ✍

Mr. Balanchine rehearses the New York City Opera and the students of the School of American Ballet in Dido and Aeneas.

*George Jackson figure-skated as a child in Vienna in the 1930s and grew up to write about dance for general publications (*Washington Star, Washington Post, Times of London*) and specialty magazines (*Dance Magazine, Ballet Review, DanceView, Ballettanz*). He served as a super in the Chicago performances of Verdi's* Aida *that George Balanchine choreographed for New York City Opera in 1948.*

A Man for All Seasons

By Clive Barnes

It did not seem like history at the time—but history never does. On October 11, 1948, at the City Center of Music and Drama on West 55th Street in New York, a young dance company called Ballet Society, founded by George Balanchine and Lincoln Kirstein, made its first appearance under its new name and, in effect, new structure, New York City Ballet. The program—naturally enough all Balanchine—consisted of *Concerto Barocco, Symphony in C,* and *Orpheus.*

Of course, that was not really City Ballet's beginning, merely the final phase of its metamorphosis from chrysalis to butterfly, a process that started when Balanchine was invited by Kirstein in 1933 to come to America to form a company. With his later famous words, "But first a school," Balanchine founded the School of American Ballet. Then, in 1934 those early students, still nonprofessionals, performed Balanchine's first ballet created in America for Americans, *Serenade.* It was the beginning of what was originally called

Mr. Balanchine with Lincoln Kirstein at the opening of the second Stravinsky Festival

Mr. Balanchine

The American Ballet, and the beginnings of all the starts, false starts, and new starts that finally, in 1946, led to Ballet Society, and two years later to New York City Ballet.

City Ballet, from its very beginnings in 1933 or whenever you want to begin the beginnings, has been a classical company that has made its own classical repertory. That was Kirstein's vision and Balanchine's design. Creativity is the engine that

has always driven the company, from that opening *Serenade* on a patrician private estate in then far-off White Plains, New York, right up to the company today and beyond.

Balanchine had an unbelievably high batting average for producing novelties that turned out, in a sense unexpectedly, to be masterpieces. Most ballets (like most plays, novels, or operas) are paper tissues: important, useful, and eventually disposable. The

Mr. Balanchine gives an interview at the Wolf Trap Center for the Performing Arts in Vienna, Virginia

number of ballets that turn out to be linen, or even lace, handkerchiefs that can be laundered and reused year after year is, of necessity, small. The metaphor is coarse and graceless, but apt. Yet Balanchine and Jerome Robbins, who eventually joined him as City Ballet's other Founding Choreographer, have together managed to leave an enormous heritage repertory. Many of the Balanchine works in that repertory are memorably encapsulated, both in style and spirit, in Costas's remarkable, timeless images of time-shot dance moments that constitute this jigsaw portrait of Balanchine's achievement and genius.

But who is Balanchine? Or rather what was he before he became a ballet icon caught between being an inspiration (the most important influence that ballet has ever known) and an industry (the creator of the world's most widely distributed repertory of ballets). Of Georgian heritage, this icon was born Georgi Melitonovich Balanchivadze in St. Petersburg, Russia, on January 22, 1904. He died George Balanchine in New York City on April 30, 1983. Between those dates lies much of ballet history.

Balanchine started his dance training at what was then the Petrograd Ballet School in 1914 and graduated in 1921. He then became a member of GATOB, which was the accepted abbreviation for Gosudarstvenny Akademichesky Teatr Opery i Baleta (State Academic Theatre for Opera and

Mr. Balanchine rehearses Rudolf Nureyev in Le Bourgeois Gentilhomme

Mr. Balanchine with Merrill Brockway, Emil Ardolino, and Twyla Tharp on the set of Prodigal Son on WNET

Ballet), which, when St. Petersburg was Petrograd before it became Leningrad before it reverted to St. Petersburg, is what the Maryinsky Ballet was called before it was called the Kirov Ballet before it reverted to the Maryinsky Ballet. No wonder Balanchivadze changed his name.

Even before he graduated into the company, he had tried his hand at choreography as a student, and now he started to study music intensively—his brother became a famous Georgian composer—and for a time seriously considered a career as a concert pianist. But slowly his interests in dance and music fused into an intent to master the craft of choreography. In 1920 he had already participated in Fyodor Lopukhov's Evenings of Young Ballet, and he came under the influence of a new generation of Russian choreographers—not only Lopukhov himself, but also more particularly Kasyan Goleizovsky.

Mr. Balanchine rehearses the "Waltz of the Flowers" from The Sleeping Beauty

In 1924 he headed a small troupe calling itself Soviet State Dancers on a tour of Germany. Once out of the Soviet Union they auditioned for the great expatriate Russian impresario, Serge Diaghilev, and most of them, including Balanchivadze (he changed his name chez Diaghilev), Tamara Geva (the first of Balanchine's four wives), and Alexandra Danilova, joined the Diaghilev Ballets Russes and stayed with the company until its dissolution upon Diaghilev's death in 1929. And, of course, it was with Diaghilev that Balanchine found his choreographic wings, creating his first two masterpieces, *Apollo* (June 12, 1928), which first brought him into contact with his lifelong friend, Igor Stravinsky, and *Prodigal Son* (May 21, 1929).

With the breakup of the Ballets Russes, Balanchine and his then-mistress Danilova found themselves at a loss. Balanchine soon found temporary work with the Paris Opera Ballet, the

Mr. Balanchine with Gordon Boelzner on the set of Noah and the Ark

Mr. Balanchine discusses his career with an interviewer

Mr. Balanchine hams it up for the camera

Mr. Balanchine with Christopher d'Amboise, Ronald Bates and John Taras

Royal Danish Ballet, and finally René Blum's newly formed Ballet Russe de Monte Carlo, the first of a number of efforts to restore the glory of Diaghilev. Falling out with that company's chief choreographer, Léonide Massine, in 1933 Balanchine became the artistic director of a small, short-lived but influential company, Les Ballets 1933, which played brief seasons in Paris and London. It was here that he met Lincoln Kirstein, who was looking for someone to head up an "American national company." His original choice was Balanchine's eternal rival, Massine, but slowly he came around to the idea of inviting Balanchine, who at that time was quite happily ensconced in London, working largely on musicals and revues, mostly for British producer Charles Cochran.

But the New World beckoned. Kirstein was persuasive—particularly after he had managed to raise the additional money needed from friends in New York—and finally Balanchine, with his manager Vladimir Dimitriev, who was to administer Balanchine's demand for (first) a school, arrived in New York Harbor aboard the *S.S. Olympic* on October 18, 1933. The rest is history (a not always untroubled history), New York City Ballet, and the ever-present subtext to this present book. ༄

Clive Barnes is a London-born New Yorker. He has been watching dance for more than sixty years and writing about it professionally for more than fifty. He has been dance critic of The Times *(London), and Chief Drama and Dance Critic of* The New York Times. *He is currently Senior Drama and Dance Critic of* The New York Post.

Fifty Great Ballets

Wendy Whelan, Jock Soto, Arch Higgins, Albert Evans, Peter Boal, Margaret Tracey, Kathleen Tracey

Agon

PREMIERE: DECEMBER 1, 1957
COMPANY: NEW YORK CITY BALLET
THEATER: CITY CENTER OF MUSIC AND DRAMA, NEW YORK

By Arthur Mitchell

In 1957 Betty Cage, the General Manager of New York City Ballet, called me to say that Mr. Balanchine would begin working on a new ballet; I would be dancing with Diana Adams. Two weeks after Betty's call, we started rehearsing *Agon*.

Agon was the third part of a trilogy begun by George Balanchine and Igor Stravinsky. The first was *Apollo*, which was premiered in Paris in 1928 by Diaghilev's Ballets Russes.

Although *Agon* was based upon many of the court dances, in my opinion, it is the definitive ballet of the neoclassical style. In fact, it set the standard for neoclassical dance today. But, what none of us realized back then was that *Agon* was also a defining moment in the history of classical ballet. It represented a major step—not only technically and musically but because it may have been one of the first ballets created for a Caucasian woman and an African-American man, me.

What is most fascinating and illustrative of Mr. Balanchine's genius is how the color of our skins was woven into the choreography. When Diana and I crossed our arms. When I embraced her. Mr. Balanchine was explicit about how the brown of my skin interface with the white of hers. It wasn't just the steps; it was the juxtaposition of this interracial couple.

Think back to the time that *Agon* premiered. In 1957 it was rare to have interracial couples dancing together in classical ballet. After it was completed, Mr. Balanchine said "this pas de deux has taken me longer than anything I have ever choreographed because it must be perfect."

The word *agon* means "competition." Therefore, within the framework of the ballet there are competitions between the individual dancers and between groups of dancers—groups against groups, quartets against trios, trios against couples. Even between the pas de deux, pas de trois, and pas de quatre, there was competition.

The process of making *Agon* was intriguing. The score had not been completed when we started. Stravinsky was living in Los Angeles and working on the music there. Each time he finished one page of music, he mailed the page to Mr. Balanchine. We went as far as we could each time a new page arrived, but we could only go so far until Mr. Stravinsky completed and mailed the next page . . . then the next page . . . and the next.

We rehearsed *Agon* to the piano score but had no idea what the orchestration would be. When we heard the full orchestral score at our dress rehearsal, it was like another world. What you thought you could relate to was no longer there. Mr. Stravinsky had added pulsing syncopation, using the dancers as another instrument. It wasn't the traditional score we were accustomed to following. Needless to say, we were all extremely nervous about opening night. But we managed to pull through.

Today, musicians find *Agon* one of the most difficult scores to play and dancers find it equally difficult to dance. When musicians have to play it, they are in absolute panic because it isn't easy to get the essence of it. They think it is a cacophony of sounds. Once they hear and understand the jazz beneath it, it becomes easy. After a while, I was able to

Darcey Bussell of the Royal Ballet (U.K.) and Lindsay Fischer

understand the timing and syncopation because I had studied tap. So I became one of the leaders, knowing what to do and at what point in the music.

The wonderful collaborative relationship that existed between Mr. Balanchine and Mr. Stravinsky became evident when Mr. Stravinsky finally arrived to see the completed piece. It was also very evident that theirs was a perfect union between two great artists. The respect and admiration that I had for Mr. Balanchine, he had in equal measure and more for Mr. Stravinsky. For me, Mr. Balanchine was the epitome of dance and choreography. To see his great admiration of Stravinsky's musical genius was really quite fascinating.

During my entire career at New York City Ballet, I had never seen or heard anyone criticize or suggest changes to Mr. Balanchine's work. However, at the end of the first pas de trois, there is an elongated port de bras. Mr. Stravinsky suggested the movement be syncopated rather than elongated and broken into separate pieces. The dancers should be doing the syncopation to the extended music. Well, I was taken aback. But after Mr. Stravinsky's suggestion was incorporated, it seemed the most natural and logical way to go.

Before *Agon* was incorporated, we didn't think that audiences would understand it; it was so different. We were also concerned about presenting it during matinees; children would never be able to relate to it. But it turned out to be a masterpiece. And to our surprise children understood it completely—in fact, much better than the adults had. Whenever and wherever we performed *Agon*, it was a great success. Even today, the pas de deux is considered one of the most inventive pieces of choreography. And I am proud to say that it was also the piece that established me as a premier dancer.

Patricia Barker and Jeffrey Stanton of Pacific Northwest Ballet

Mr. Balanchine had a genius for working on four ballets simultaneously; that was well known. It was also known that he could sit at a piano and play the music, he could sing it, and he could also "hear" the orchestration. He was also a master at knowing what looked good on a dancer's body and what movement could extend a dancer's body.

Mr. Balanchine often incorporated natural movement from the street. During rehearsals for *Serenade*, his first ballet in America, one of the dancers arrived late and came rushing breathless into the studio. Mr. Balanchine said "Beautiful! Keep that in." One morning when he arrived for rehearsal on *Agon*, it was clear that his knee was bothering him. He was limping. He added the limp to the choreography. The "toe, flat," "toe, flat" step that the boys do came out of that day.

Fifty years later, *Agon* still stands very much on its own and in a class by itself. No matter how many times you see it, something fresh and new and provocative can be discovered. Equally important, *Agon* literally helped change the face of classical ballet. New York City Ballet's dancers, including an interracial couple, helped bring to life a treasure trove of pure choreographic and musical genius and in doing so one of the most important landmarks of dance was established. ◡

Darcey Bussell from the Royal Ballet (U.K.), and Lindsay Fischer from the New York City Ballet

Arthur Mitchell is an accomplished artistic director, astute educator, talented choreographer, and extraordinary dancer. In 1955, he was the first African-American male to become a permanent member of a major ballet company when he joined the New York City Ballet. During his fifteen-year career with New York City Ballet, Mitchell rose quickly to the rank of Principal Dancer and electrified audiences with his performances in a spectrum of roles. In 1969, Mitchell founded Dance Theatre of Harlem with his mentor and ballet teacher Karel Shook and now serves as director of the organization.

Suzanne Farrell and Peter Martins

Wendy Whelan from the New York City Ballet and Donald Williams from the Dance Theater of Harlem

Peter Boal, Zipora Karz, and Catherine Tracey

Sofia Gumerova, Igor Zelensky, Daria Pavlenko, Veronika Part of the Kirov Ballet

Apollo

PREMIERE: NOVEMBER 15, 1951
COMPANY: NEW YORK CITY BALLET
THEATER: CITY CENTER OF MUSIC AND DRAMA

by Peter Martins

Mr. Balanchine rehearses before the show

A is for apple. When we are children, that is how our lessons begin. When you are a dancer, however, A is for *Apollo*. That is true no matter which country or ballet tradition shapes you. I was unaware of this in 1967, but it was something I was soon to learn.

That year I was no longer a child. I was twenty-one in 1967. Having joined the Royal Danish Ballet three years earlier, I had just been named a Principal Dancer. Invitations to perform as a guest artist were starting to show up, and outside choreographers were interested in working with me. My faith that I knew what I was doing seemed to be confirmed by the evidence around me. If I needed more proof, that spring I was given the role of Apollo to learn. It was a great honor. My uncle, Leif Ørnberg, had been the first Dane to dance the role in 1930, when George Balanchine let the Royal Danish

Peter Martins as Apollo

Nikolaj Hübbe as Apollo

Igor Zelensky of the Kirov Ballet

Ballet have the ballet shortly after its creation in 1928. If you had asked me then about my vision of myself as a dancer, I would have responded with all the certainty of youth and 20/20 sight, blissfully unaware of the myopia clouding my eyes.

In some sense, you might say I was "saved by the bell." In my case, the ring of a telephone when the call came looking for an emergency replacement to dance *Apollo* at New York City Ballet's 1967 Edinburgh Festival opening-night performance in two days' time. Confident that the NYCB had found the right guy and that I could meet any challenge, I headed off to meet Balanchine.

As a dancer, one is privileged to see many magical moments that audiences do not get to share. Sometimes it is a moment of inspiration or breakthrough, or a perfect performance during practice. The day I met Balanchine was one of those times. It was in a rehearsal studio, where Balanchine asked Suzanne Farrell, who was cast as Terpsichore

Mr. Balanchine rehearses Jean-Pierre Frohlich, Patricia McBride, Stephanie Saland, and Elyse Borne

Mr. Balanchine rehearses Patricia McBride

for the upcoming performance, and me to dance the pas de deux. We did. He watched. He did not say anything. Then he took off his jacket and proceeded to dance *Apollo*'s variations. In an instant, I felt like a kid again. Not only had I been outdanced by a man in his early sixties, but, more importantly, I could see I would have to learn my ABCs all over again.

I had always known that *Apollo* was "about" the rites of passage required of us all. Only then—as an audience of one—did I come to understand its true subject is receptivity, which is the foundation of all great dancing. In the gift of a single performance, a whole new world opened up to me. That day in Edinburgh, my lessons had just begun. ᴗ

Peter Martins is Ballet Master in Chief of New York City Ballet and Chairman of the Faculty at the School of American Ballet.

Mr. Balanchine rehearses Stephanie Saland

Peter Martins and Kyra Nichols

Nina Ananiashvili and Andris Liepa of the Bolshoi Ballet

Mikhail Baryshnikov

Daria Pavlenko and Yana Serebriakova of the Kirov Ballet

Mikhail Baryshnikov

Mr. Balanchine rehearses Stephanie Saland

Ib Andersen

Margaret Tracey performs a solo

Ballo della Regina

PREMIERE: JANUARY 12, 1941
COMPANY: NEW YORK CITY BALLET
THEATER: NEW YORK STATE THEATER, NEW YORK

by Merrill Ashley

Merrill Ashley and Robert Weiss

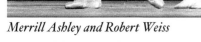

Merrill Ashley and Robert Weiss

In October 1977 one of my lifelong dreams came true when George Balanchine told me he was going to choreograph a ballet for me—a virtuoso ballet. He said he would use the ballet music from Verdi's opera *Don Carlos*. Although this was to be a plotless ballet, he told me the story in the libretto, which was about a fisherman searching underwater for a perfect pearl to put in the crown of the Queen of Spain. When he began to choreograph, I realized he had used that story to give him inspiration for patterns of movement, such as waves of people moving on the stage and certain port de bras motifs that were related to swimming. The entrances for both principal dancers that lead into the pas de deux also have an air of searching, although it is not clear what they are looking for.

Balanchine suggested to the lighting and costume designers that they try to create a look related to mother-of-pearl in their designs. Dappled costumes were designed in various shades of white, pink, and lavender, and an inventive way was found to reflect light, in the same colors, onto the backdrop that produced a similar dappled effect. The result was that the whole ballet took on the iridescent look of mother-of-pearl.

It took Balanchine only one week to choreograph the ballet. He started with the pas de deux and then did the solos for Robert Weiss and me. It was clear in both my solos that speed was a critical element in the virtuosity he had in mind. There were jumps on pointe and lots of intricate footwork for me, as well as many different types of pas de chat, including an original variation that he put in my second solo, and never again used in his choreography. Robert Weiss's

Merrill Ashley soars on stage

Miranda Weese and Damian Woetzel

solos were filled with multiple pirouettes, beats, and traditional male virtuoso jumps, also done at a faster tempo than usual. Everything he choreographed for us suited us perfectly, both technically and stylistically, while giving us the opportunity to show our joy of dancing throughout the ballet.

Next, Balanchine choreographed the solos for the four soloist girls. He then "created" the opening and finale of the ballet, leaving the middle section for the corps de ballet for last. (Balanchine refused to use the word "create" about his work. "God creates, I assemble," he often said.) I was amazed that he could jump about like this, never appearing confused or at a loss for ideas. As he progressed he seemed more and more pleased with his work. In fact, during run-through rehearsals, after the ballet was completed, he would often, so uncharacteristically, just sit in his chair with a Cheshire-cat grin on his face, obviously delighted with what he had done and how it was being danced.

Once the ballet was complete, I could not help but feel that Balanchine had treated me like his "perfect pearl," setting me in his crown of beautiful choreography. This was a ballet meant to highlight my skills, quite unlike *Ballade*, which he later choreographed for me to help me grow and become a more complete artist.

I have always felt that *Ballo* is the best curtain raiser in the New York City Ballet repertory. It makes everyone forget the stresses of life, as it fills the audience and the dancers with its buoyant spirit, its energy, and the joy of life and dancing. ᴄ⅃ᴏ

Merrill Ashley is a former Principal Dancer with the New York City Ballet, and is currently part of the artistic staff at New York City Ballet as the Teaching Associate. She also stages Balanchine ballets for the George Balanchine Trust and gives lectures about Balanchine and his ballets for the George Balanchine Foundation.

Miranda Weese performs a solo

Maria Kowroski

Benjamin Millepied

Brahms-Schoenberg Quartet

PREMIERE: APRIL 21, 1966
COMPANY: NEW YORK CITY BALLET
THEATER: NEW YORK STATE THEATER, NEW YORK

By Colleen Neary

The *Brahms–Schoenberg Quartet* cannot be defined as one ballet, but as four ballets within one. With each movement portraying a difference in style and mood, it lends itself to the viewer's palate, similar to a four-course meal finishing with a grand dessert. Having danced three of the four movements, I have a personal relationship with it, but I would also like to describe it from an audience's view.

The first movement, Allegro, with its full corps de ballet, solo woman, and principal couple is a complete ballet and would serve as an "opener" on any program. From the outset, its beauty is evident in the patterns, structure, musicality, and energy. It builds with repeated entrances of a vibrant solo woman and four men and stands solid with the several pas de deux of the principal couple. Performing the role of the solo woman early in my career was very exciting and energizing. The beauty and musicality of the choreography has a grand and regal feeling.

The second movement, Intermezzo, built around a center couple and three female demi-soloists, is a small piece of Romanticism. Again, the beauty of this ballet is expressed through its Romantic quality. The breath of the movement is light and like a cloud that never seems to touch ground. The three women are the wind running and dancing around and through the center couple. The pas de deux, although technically quite demanding, has the ease that only Balanchine could so masterfully achieve.

The third movement, Andante, is elegant and regal in its demeanor. A center couple is the focal point, surrounded by three solo women and a corps of twelve women. Its pas de deux and solos have a certain lyricism and classicism that refer back to Balanchine's upbringing and training in Imperial Russia. I enjoyed tremendously dancing this classic pas de deux as part

New York City Ballet

of the center couple with Adam Lüders. With the freedom that Balanchine's choreography has in its style and movement, it leaves you with a sense of fulfillment and joy as both a dancer and a viewer.

Last, but definitely not least, is the fourth movement, Rondo alla Zingarese. Its feeling in costumes, choreography, and mood is gypsy. Wild and exhilarating would describe this section. Completely different again in style, it leaves you on the edge of your seat with excitement. The lead couple is surrounded by twelve couples dancing a spirited and sensual dance together, climaxing continually to the last note. Dancing as part of the twelve couples, and later in my career as the lead woman with my husband, Thordal Christensen, in the Pacific Northwest Ballet, was probably the most fun I have had in my dancing career. The music carries you to the end and the choreography is so organic in its structure it sings along. This could be called the perfect ending to a perfect ballet.

Colleen Neary was trained at the School of American Ballet and Harkness House. She danced as a soloist with the New York City Ballet from 1969–1979. She also served as a faculty member of the School of American Ballet and company teacher. Ms. Neary was ballet mistress for The Zurich Ballet from 1979–1984 and principal guest artist with Maurice Bejart's Ballet du Deuxieme Siecle from 1984–1986. From 1986–1992 she danced with Pacific Northwest Ballet as a Principal Dancer and was the First Ballet Mistress for The Royal Danish Ballet from 1992–2002. Ms. Neary is a member of The George Balanchine Trust and stages Balanchine ballets around the world.

Colleen Neary, flanked by Victor Castelli, David Richardson, and Peter Nauman

Monique Meunier

Suzanne Farrell and Peter Martins in a classic scene from Chaconne

Chaconne

Premiere: January 22, 1976
Company: New York City Ballet
Theater: New York State Theater, New York

By Joel Lobenthal

Chaconne is a jubilant ballet that harbors an elegiac note of farewell. Balanchine made it seven years before his death, and it was his final response to Gluck's 1762 *Orpheus and Eurydice,* an opera based on myth detailing a return to the Underworld that had interested Balanchine for decades. In 1936 he staged Gluck's *Orpheus* at the Metropolitan Opera; in 1963 he choreographed a production at the Hamburg Opera and then in 1973 another production at the Paris Opera. In *Chaconne*, he used a suite of musical excerpts written for dance interludes in the opera. There was a hallowed choreographic pedigree attached: the great choreographer Jean-Georges Noverre had created dances for the Stuttgart production during the 1760s.

After *Chaconne*'s ballerina and her cavalier first appear from opposite corners of the stage, their duet to music written for the Dance of the Blessed Spirits

Suzanne Farrell and Peter Martins

Judith Fugate and Peter Boal

eschews the pirouettes or high lifts of a classical adagio. It is a reminder of the importance of plastique in Balanchine's work. By plastique I mean the shapes the body assumes, as opposed to the ability of the legs to negotiate quantities of intricate steps. The white costumes and blue background suggest seas, clouds, and horizon. Their serene demeanor and the lack of vehemence in their movement suggest a stroll through the empyrean.

After the leads vanish, the mood changes. We are treated to a pas de trois, in which three new dancers perform a hip-swinging walk that is a loving yet irreverent look at the posing and parading of court dances in vogue when *Orpheus* was composed. Then a pas de deux by another couple, who flashes the flat palms of the jester's shrug of insouciance. Now a petite young woman appears with her retinue, like a flock of rococo shepherdesses.

When the ballerina and her partner return, they dance a minuet. There are repeats of the softly pedaling legs of the opening adagio, now performed to an entirely different meter.

In the gavotte that follows, the man and woman dance to a theme and variations structure; performing purling variations that tumble over each other like breakers on the beach. It is as though they are truly dancing circles around each other.

Chaconne remains a portrait of its original ballerina, Suzanne Farrell, although the work has survived handily in the performances of successive interpreters. Farrell had a pronounced affinity for plastique, as well as the kinetic ability to tap into, and yet transcend, her American cultural inheritance. In *Chaconne* she was deliciously droll. She drew linkages between the grandiloquent processional of the rococo and the cheeky strut of the drum majorette.

Throughout the ballet the choreographic lexicon goes from dreamy and celestial to earthy and prankish. Balanchine closes his ballet as Gluck did his opera, with a final chaconne, in which the two principal dancers lead a surging, celebratory ensemble. Balanchine's choreography is now at its most signature neoclassicism, a unique, synthesized, yet autonomous vocabulary. We in the audience are reminded anew of the ways that the art of ballet, born in the Renaissance, was now proceeding apace by the time Gluck composed *Orpheus.* As the decades leapt forward to Balanchine's era, ballet increasingly became an independent vocabulary, yet still aware and indebted, and perhaps inextricably tied, to court entertainments of the past. ໒

Joel Lobenthal is assistant editor of Ballet Review. *He has also written for* Playbill, Stagebill, Quest, Dance Magazine, *and* The New York Times. *ReganBooks is publishing his biography of Tallulah Bankhead in 2004.*

Suzanne Farrell and Peter Martins

Maria Kowroski and Charles Askegaard

Concerto Barocco

PREMIERE: JUNE 27, 1941
COMPANY: AMERICAN BALLET CARAVAN
THEATER: TEATRO MUNICIPAL, RIO DE JANEIRO

By Barbara Weisberger

January 22, 2004, is the 100th anniversary of George Balanchine's birthday, and beyond any previous plaudits, he will be commemorated in hundreds of ways by thousands of individuals and groups. One hundred years probably is less incredible to me than most others. My father died on January 24, 2002, three months short of his 101st birthday, and counting on the transference of his genes has to a large degree kept me removed from any looming sense of my own mortality. However, my hopeful personal allusions to mortality have little bearing on the widely shared conviction that (certainly in a non-fleshly sense) Balanchine is immortal. Even among those who were not admirers of his ballets, he was considered at least the rarest of geniuses and greatest of choreographers.

Could I have laughed and cried with, been kissed on the cheek and comforted by, the lovely man who in two or three hundred years from now will unquestionably be perceived as Mozart is today? As time passes, the true dilemma for me, and I suspect for those like me who knew Balanchine more than casually (usually signified by the immunity to call him Mr. B), is the ability—or willingness—to separate the man from the god. The man-god confusion was an enigma: the disarming simplicity, seemingly pubescent ingenuousness of the man was constantly present within the awesome god who quietly inspired complete and reverential admiration. Our communication was often intimidating, sometimes tantalizing, and always very much alive.

On the other hand, Balanchine's ballets—his god-like assemblages—were not enigmatic. They (not all, but most) were truth: organisms, pieces of life, and like life. They were made up of moments, some soaring, some still, but mostly somewhere in the vast territory in between. Many Balanchine ballets contained not one but several wondrously perfect moments, and one was sure there was no imaginable way they could be improved.

In the process of rehearsal as well as in

performance, a Balanchine work was, and in most cases still is, my greatest source of aesthetic joy and enlightenment. For more reasons than the ballet's intrinsic beauty, that response is never more palpable than in the case of *Concerto Barocco*. The work, originally set in 1941 to Bach's Concerto for Two Violins, was the first ballet Balanchine chose to offer the fledgling Pennsylvania Ballet for its first

The cast of the New York City Ballet

Philadelphia performance in 1964. Four years later, with chutzpah and unflagging optimism, it was the opening ballet of the company's first major New York appearance, a week-long season at City Center. Despite the dancers' jittery nerves, the performance was a gratifying success.

If any ballet could have been called a Pennsylvania Ballet signature piece, it was *Concerto Barocco*, from the first stamina-building rehearsals, led by our great ballet master, Robert Rodham, at the old Chestnut Street studio, when the dancers, after the third excruciating run-through, would fall into a heap of red-faced, sweaty, and heaving bodies, to a "once-in-a-lifetime," show-stopping performance at the Brooklyn Academy of Music in the mid-1970s, when everything came magically together and the applause (and tears) came down like rain, to recent performances, probably danced with easier virtuosity, but certainly not with more love. The qualities within *Concerto Barocco* are, in essence, metaphors for Balanchine, the artist and the man: logic, ingenuity, elegance, harmony, grandeur, good manners, lack of artifice, and generosity—always generosity.

It was Balanchine's incredible generosity, wise counsel, and moral support that truly reinforced the course of my professional life. For almost fifty years, interweaving through the evolving tapestry of indigenous American ballet, my dance life touched or at least skirted around the fringes of Balanchine's, from the eight-year-old child watching with wonder as he first taught *Serenade* to the father,

Margaret Tracey and Kathleen Tracey

Merrill Ashley (center) and dancers from the New York City Ballet

savior, and loyal friend role he played in the formation of the Pennsylvania Ballet, and much more. At the traumatic and painful end of my Pennsylvania Ballet days in February 1982, a year before he died, Mr. B called me to his office to meet with him, an extraordinary gesture considering that for quite a few years some of my choices had sorely disappointed him. (He knew they were wrong well before I did.) When I arrived, he reached for my hand, and as he patted it, he said, "We will start all over again. We will do *Concerto Barocco* with a lovely chamber orchestra. It will be all right, don't worry." My tears flowed as they often did in the early years of the Pennsylvania Ballet, when his kindnesses overwhelmed me and my "pussycats" (the name he called my hungry, loving first dancers, Barbara Sandonato and Patricia Turko) while we were holding on with bloody fingernails. ❧

Barbara Weisberger, visionary leader, inspiring teacher and artistic director, and founder of the Pennsylvania Ballet, has been in the vanguard of every important movement of contemporary American ballet. At the age of eight, she was the first child accepted at Balanchine's School of American Ballet and began a long career in dance. She culminated her distinguished career with the conception in 1984 of the Carlisle Project, the distinctive, highly respected national program for the professional development of choreographers and dancers, which she led until the end of 1996 when the Project's formal operations were suspended. Since Spring 2001, she has been Artistic Advisor of Peabody Dance.

Kyra Nichols and Lourdes Lopez

Gelsey Kirkland and Conrad Ludlow

Nicole Hlinka and Damian Woetzel

Coppélia

PREMIERE: JULY 17, 1974
COMPANY: NEW YORK CITY BALLET
THEATER: SARATOGA PERFORMING ARTS CENTER, SARATOGA SPRINGS, NEW YORK

by Mary Cargill

The premiere of Balanchine's version of the 1870 French ballet starred Patricia McBride as Swanilda, Helgi Tomasson as Franz, and Shaun O'Brien as the deluded Dr. Coppélius. Balanchine and Alexandra Danilova, who was responsible for setting Act II of the Balanchine version, had both danced in the pre-Revolution *Coppélia* as students in Russia. (The choreographer of that version, Marius Petipa, had seen the original French version some ten years after its premiere and had created his own version for the Maryinsky Ballet in 1884.) Danilova, of course, was a world-famous Swanilda in the 1940s and 1950s with the Ballet Russe, whose version also derived from Petipa's. So Balanchine's *Coppélia*, especially the wonderful second act with its mime and character dancing, is based solidly in the nineteenth century.

Balanchine loved Delibes's music for its lilt and infectious melodies. The music was much richer and more varied than the usual ballet scores of the time; Delibes had traveled to Hungary and studied the country's folk music, and *Coppélia* was the first ballet score to incorporate the mazurka. Balanchine's choreography in Act I keeps the folk flavor of the music.

Helgi Tomasson performs a solo while the cast of the New York City Ballet looks on

Shaun O'Brien and Nicole Hlinka

Margaret Tracey

The dramatic details were also important to Balanchine. In an interview, Judith Fugate described Balanchine carefully rehearsing her as the friend of Swanilda who finds the key to Dr. Coppélius's house at the end of Act I: "We got to the part with the key. All the friends were standing around, and he said, 'Well now, someone has to find the key.' And he looked around and said, 'Judy, Judy the actress,' and he showed me exactly how I had to pick it up and look at it and show it so the whole audience could see what it was, and then do the whole action/reaction thing. He was very careful about those details and wanted to be sure the story was clear."

Balanchine choreographed all of Delibes's allegorical variations in Act III. The twenty-four girls who open the act are the Golden Hours, who make up the day. They are also acts of homage and a continuation of the Imperial Russian tradition of using ballet students in productions, both to give the productions variety and to provide the students with stage experience. The variations Dawn, Prayer, and the Spinner signifying work represent various human activities; Discord and War (the Wagnerian Valkyries) are vanquished by Peace, in the form of the lovers' pas de deux, for which Balanchine interpolated music from Delibes's *La Source* for Franz's solo.

Coppélia's past is graciously acknowledged in the designs by Rouben Ter-Arutunian, whose bells in the final act include the initials of Arthur Saint-Léon, the original choreographer, and Charles Nuitter, who devised the joyful libretto. ❧

Mary Cargill, a librarian at Columbia University, has been writing about dance for ten years. Her articles and reviews have appeared in DanceView, Ballet Alert, Ballet Review, *and other publications.*

Patricia McBride and Shaun O'Brien

Stephanie Saland and Peter Martins

Sofia Gumerova of the Kirov Ballet

Diamonds

PREMIERE: APRIL 13, 1967
COMPANY: NEW YORK CITY BALLET
THEATER: NEW YORK STATE THEATER, NEW YORK

By Caitlin Sims

The seductive brilliance of diamonds—clear, multifaceted, and everlasting—infuses the third section of Balanchine's *Jewels*. The dancers sparkle in intricately jewel-encrusted white tutus and tiaras, refracting light with every delicate turn and jump. A kaleidoscopic glitter from thirty-four exquisitely coordinated dancers creates a mesmerizing intensity similar to gazing into the heart of a dazzling stone.

Despite the shimmering effects of the costumes and lighting, the enduring luster of *Diamonds* lies in its radiant choreography. Instead of creating a narrative or a literal evocation of a precious gem, Balanchine decided to illuminate the essence of diamonds through a tribute to the opulent refinement of tsarist

Russia. Courtly and elegant, the movement hearkens back to the grandeur of the Imperial Ballet of St. Petersburg, whose traditions Balanchine inherited with his childhood training. The principles and conventions of Maryinsky Ballet choreographer Marius Petipa are translated to a plotless work; his vision of ideal love is expressed with the same respectful formality, yet the interweaving steps are subtly altered so that they are entirely new.

Balanchine set his homage to Imperial Russia to sections of Tchaikovsky's sweeping and majestic Symphony No. 3 in D Major, which Tchaikovsky completed just before *Swan Lake*. The ballet opens with a waltz for twelve women followed by a central

Kyra Nichols

Suzanne Farrell and Peter Martins

pas de deux, a scherzo with displays of bravura technique, and a grand polonaise, in which sixteen corps de ballet couples join the principals for an effervescent finale. There are visual references to Petipa's choreography for *Swan Lake:* the Swan Queen Odette, with her purity, innocence, and vulnerability, is evoked repeatedly in *Diamonds* as the ballerina's wrists meet above her head and again as she bends backward, supported at the waist by her partner.

Balanchine created the lengthy pas de deux for his muse, Suzanne Farrell, with Jacques d'Amboise as her devoted partner. The pair enters from opposite sides of the stage with a simple walk encompassing the elegant propriety of courtly manners. Despite their aristocratic decorum, there is a tenderness and passion between the dancers; it is the careful attention of the danseur that enables the ballerina to revel in soaring leaps, sweeping turns, and deep falls into his arms.

Suzanne Farrell and Peter Martins

Lindsay Fischer and Kyra Nichols

The full-length *Jewels* (which also includes *Emeralds* and *Rubies*) was created in 1967 for New York City Ballet's first season in the spacious New York State Theater at Lincoln Center, and the scale of the movement crafted for the long-limbed Farrell is equally expansive. Yet the plunging arabesques and soaring lifts lead to a moment that is deeply resonant because of its sweet simplicity. As the pas de deux comes to a close, the male dancer kneels and gently kisses his partner's left hand, sealing their union in the same place that a ring—often a diamond—symbolizes love and commitment. ✿

Caitlin Sims is editorial director of Dance Spirit *and* Dance Teacher *magazines and a freelance writer.*

Mr. Balanchine rehearses Suzanne Farrell and Peter Martins

Suzanne Farrell and Peter Martins perform a duet

Merrill Ashley

Divertimento #15

PREMIERE: MAY 31, 1956
COMPANY: NEW YORK CITY BALLET
THEATER: MOZART FESTIVAL, AMERICAN SHAKESPEARE THEATRE, STRATFORD, CONNECTICUT

by Nancy Goldner

"The Mozart of choreography" is how Balanchine is often described. It so happens, though, that Balanchine composed to only a few Mozart scores (most of them incidental dances for opera), and of those few, one is a repeat: the Divertimento No. 15 in E-flat Major. The first ballet, made in 1952, had the lovely title *Caracole* and was created for a Mozart festival in Stratford, Connecticut. The steps were quickly forgotten, however, but the music apparently continued to grip Balanchine's imagination because four years later he made a new ballet to the same music. This one, happily, survives.

It also happens that this Mozart ballet is quite un-Mozartian in terms of its numerical construction. Cast for five ballerinas and three cavaliers, it is decidedly unsymmetrical. How Balanchine works through this odd-lot assortment of leading characters is one of the fascinations of the ballet. Most of the time one is not aware of the unconventionality of the scheme, but there is one passage where Balanchine brings the issue to the fore, to face it head on. This daring passage occurs in the long cadenza toward the end of the andante, which Balanchine stages as a slowly unfolding series of tableaux in which the ballerinas are supported by the men. Despite the uneven breakdown of men and women, Balanchine

Tracey Bennett, Susan Pilarre, Maria Calegari, Merrill Ashley, Robert Weiss, Stephanie Saland, Marjorie Spohn, Victor Castelli

Margaret Illman of the National Ballet (Canada)

creates a world of perfect equanimity by letting the five women take turns being partnered in their développés and promenades. The momentarily single ladies retire to the background, but the continuum of exchange between foreground and background and between the three gents and their ladies ensures the illusion of inclusion. It is a sublime resolution to the five-and-three "problem."

While no other sections of *Divertimento No. 15* are as conceptually exciting as this, the ballet is a beauty through and through. The theme and variations section, which is introduced by a stunning legato passage for two of the three male dancers and followed by six variations for the women and lead cavalier, is delightful for its slightly contrasting personalities. The sixth variation is the showiest because it is the quickest. The New York City Ballet's more intelligent ballerinas have traditionally had fun commenting on the wit of the solo. They finish either with a grand flourish, as if to say, "There, I've done it!" or they end with a tiny shrug: "Oh, it was nothing at all."

But it is the andante that takes one's breath away. Although it is a series of five separate pas de deux (one for each of the women), it flows along as if on one

Mr. Balanchine rehearses Victor Castelli

Mr. Balanchine rehearses Merrill Ashley and Robert Weiss

breath. Although each duet has a slightly different coloration, the effect is not one of contrast, as in the theme and variations, but of eternal continuity. The andante does not go on forever, however; indeed, Balanchine makes a point of the finiteness of musical time. At the very end, the women and men each gather in a circle on opposite sides of the stage. Each raises an arm toward the center of their two circles, as if to offer a toast to the beautiful music—and perhaps to acknowledge the end of their journey. Then they bow to the group on the other side of the expanse and exit in opposite directions. Endings are sad.

But do not shed too many tears. The finale is wonderful, too. ❧

Nancy Goldner has written dance criticism for numerous publications, among them The Christian Science Monitor, The Nation, Philadelphia Inquirer, *and* The New York Times. *She currently conducts a nationwide lecture series on Balanchine for the George Balanchine Foundation.*

Philip Neal and Carla Körbes in the andante

Margaret Tracey and Ethan Stiefel

Merrill Ashley and Robert Weiss perform a duet

Helgi Tomasson

Divertimento from Baiser de la Fée

PREMIERE: JUNE 21, 1972
COMPANY: NEW YORK CITY BALLET
THEATER: STRAVINSKY FESTIVAL, NEW YORK STATE THEATER, NEW YORK

By Helgi Tomasson

This was one of the very first ballets Balanchine worked on for the 1972 Stravinsky Festival. He said he had used the music before, but he could not remember and wanted to start from the beginning and do a ballet for Patty [Patricia McBride] and me. We worked on it and I liked it a lot. There was a solo for Patty, and there was a coda for me but not really a separate solo. With Balanchine, if that was how he saw it, that was it. It would have been nice to have a solo, but if he did not feel it was right for this ballet, I accepted that.

Balanchine went on to choreograph many other ballets; all the while we were getting closer and closer to the festival. Then one day Gordon Boelzner, the pianist, saw me in the hallway and said, "We're going to work on *Baiser* again. Mr. B found some music and I think he might be doing a solo for you."

I was called to the rehearsal studio late the next day. Gordon was there. Mr. B said, "I've found some music and I want to see what I can do, maybe a solo for you." I seem to remember it was music he had used for a fortuneteller in the former version, because he said to me, "The music will be mysterious."

Mr. B had Gordon play a little bit as he started to indicate steps. I was eager to follow. I do not remember his changing anything—maybe minor things. It came so fast, it was almost hard to keep up in terms of remembering it, but we just kept going and going. I remember that we had a two-hour rehearsal scheduled. One hour and twenty minutes later, the solo was finished. Mr. B told me to take a rest and try to remember everything. After about ten minutes, he said, "Let's see it." He watched and said, "Okay, good. Now work on it, and I will take a look at it later."

Helgi Tomasson

Jeffrey Edwards

Helgi Tomasson

Nicole Hlinka and Ben Huys

And that was it, done in less than two hours. That was fast for a solo that was so unusual. I knew it was different, but I could not really envision what it would look like at that point because I was so busy trying to remember what came next as well as the timing, the phrasing, and the musicality. I was thrilled with it; it was hard, stamina-wise, and there were a lot of tricky things, such as changing directions very unexpectedly, so I really needed to work on it, and I did. Mr. B did not see the solo again until (I believe) two days before the premiere. We did the rehearsal onstage and he said, "Very good, very good," and did not change a thing. And that is how the solo in *Baiser de la Fée* came about.

The strangeness in the solo was, I think, a combination of what he was explaining to me and what I did inadvertently. He was going for a tour jeté en tournant in the air, so he said, "Then get ready to step into the next sequence." The music at that point is a little fast, so I think what happened was that when I had gone into the air and turned, it felt like I was late getting into the next step. He saw me trying to rush it, and I was in the air when I changed direction. And he said, "That's good! Yes, that works wonderfully." It was not that I invented anything; it was just how he caught the accidental movement. He said, "You go into the air, you change, change, change, and go on. Try to articulate each part of the jump and the change in direction in the air." So perhaps it came accidentally, but then he would dwell on it and refine it until it looked the way he wanted.

It was a very unusual, extremely inventive solo for a male dancer. It had soft movements, it had fast movements, it covered a lot of space, and it had a great many technical difficulties that were not very obvious; they were very understated and, like the solo itself, progressively got more difficult as it went on. You had to dance full out in rehearsal—you wanted to be sure you were really on top of it when you started; if not, your legs would give in.

Baiser is poetic. It starts that way in the first movement: when you step forward, your arms are sweeping over the floor. It is hard to tell what Mr. B had in mind; he would not explain it more than saying it was mysterious.

The ending—the last manège, those big assemblé jumps and dropping to the knee and following through with the arms—is very beautiful and soft, yet there is nothing feminine about it. Mr. B was certainly not afraid of showing the softness he obviously could feel in the music. ❧

Patricia McBride and Helgi Tomasson

Since his appointment to the position of artistic director in 1985, Helgi Tomasson has developed San Francisco Ballet from a regional troupe to a world-class company, praised for its diversity and broad repertory. Tomasson was first discovered by Jerome Robbins in his native Iceland and offered a dance scholarship to New York's School of American Ballet. Subsequently, he began his professional career with the Joffrey Ballet, the Harkness Ballet, and later joined New York City Ballet where he became one of the company's most celebrated principal dancers. Tomasson has choreographed more than thirty works. His numerous awards include being named Officier in the French Order of Arts and Letters for contributing to furtherance of the arts in France and worldwide, being named a Commander of the Order of the Falcon by the President of Iceland for his continuous achievement in the arts, and receiving an honorary doctorate from New York's Juilliard School in 2002.

Helgi Tomasson

Suzanne Farrell and Jacques d'Amboise

Don Quixote

PREMIERE: MAY 28, 1965
COMPANY: NEW YORK CITY BALLET
THEATER: NEW YORK STATE THEATER, NEW YORK

by Suzanne Farrell

Mr. B told me sometime in the early part of 1965 that he was going to make a big three-act ballet about a man who is searching for his ideal and that she was going to be me. When Nicolas Nabokov (the composer of the score) and I were introduced for the first time, he took a long, hard look at me and said, "You know, George has always wanted to do this ballet, for twenty-five years he has wanted to do this ballet, but he always said, 'I never found my Dulcinea.'" Mr. B told me the same story a few days later.

In his usual way, Mr. B did not choose to explain Dulcinea to me verbally, but he began involving me in the larger process of putting together what was to be the company's longest, most complicated, and most expensive production to date. *Don Quixote* was a rite of passage for me on many levels—on dancing "off-balance," on being a ballerina, and on being Balanchine's ballerina.

We began putting together my third-act variation and as far as I know, this was the first

actual choreography he did on the ballet. The third-act dream scene was the dancing climax of the whole ballet, and I think beginning there gave him the roots and the atmosphere for the rest; knowing where it would end told him where it might begin and where it had to go. This variation was long, the longest I had ever danced, and Mr. B probably wanted to see if I could sustain its demands, which were both technical and dramatic. "I want pulsing, pulsing," Mr. B said, and it was for me to lunge, fall, withdraw, reach out, yearn, stretch, spin, and tighten

Suzanne Farrell and Adam Lüders

Suzanne Farrell and Adam Lüders

Suzanne Farrell and Jacques d'Amboise as Dulcinea and Don Quixote

Suzanne Farrell and Jacques D'Amboise as Dulcinea and Don Quixote

with the music. In the course of these rehearsals, we first developed what came to be called my "off-balance" movement. It was to be much commented on and seen as one of my trademarks.

As in *Meditation,* I had no understudy for *Don Quixote.* The world premiere was a gala benefit on May 27, and when Mr. B told me that he was going to perform the role of the Don, perhaps I should not have been surprised, but I was. A half-hour before the curtain was to rise, he appeared backstage in full regalia. He looked wildly theatrical and seemed very much pleased with the effect. But he was also very emotional, and when you consider that he had been planning this event for so many years and that now I was part of his plan, it is no surprise that I danced that whole evening with tears in my eyes. I saw only him, nothing else. We danced entirely for each other, and in a curious way all the emotion was a relief, a release of everything that had been building up between us without any direct expression. The ballet became a kind of public courtship, a declaration, where dance, mime, and ceremony mingled with our real lives and emotions so deeply that our onstage and offstage selves became interwoven.

After the final curtain fell that first night, the applause flooded in and with it the reality of where we were; it was time to bow. Mr. B had sent me a huge bouquet of red roses, which I received onstage, and we bowed together, over and over. The ballet seemed to be well received, especially by a gala audience that traditionally sits on its hands, and no small portion of the applause was for Balanchine's performance. His appearances were rare, and here he had embodied a role that he so clearly was living, not just acting, that this night had already been marked down in the history books. ❧

Suzanne Farrell was a Principal Dancer with the New York City Ballet from 1965 to 1989, during which time George Balanchine created twenty-three ballets expressly for her. As a répétiteur for the George Balanchine Trust she has staged Balanchine ballets for the Royal Danish Ballet, the Kirov Ballet, the Bolshoi Ballet, and for companies throughout the United States. She is now artistic director of The Suzanne Farrell Ballet, the resident company of The Kennedy Center for the Performing Arts in Washington D.C. The above text is excerpted from her autobiography, Holding On to the Air.

Suzanne Farrell on pointe

Kay Mazzo and Peter Martins

Duo Concertant

PREMIERE: JUNE 22, 1972
COMPANY: NEW YORK CITY BALLET
THEATER: STRAVINSKY FESTIVAL, NEW YORK STATE THEATER, NEW YORK

by Kay Mazzo

Over dinner one night, Mr. Balanchine said he had a piece of music he wanted to choreograph. He said he loved this particular piece very much and he wanted the audience to listen and admire it too. He wanted the curtain to rise and the two musicians (Gordon Boelzner and Lamar Alsop) to play the first movement without the dancers (Peter Martins and me) moving—just listening. He said the first movement would be the hors d'oeuvre; the dancing

in the second, third, and fourth movements the main course; and the last movement the woman—the untouchable, worshipped woman—dessert.

I am sure Mr. Balanchine chose Peter not only for his dancing, but also because Peter is extremely musical and quick to learn. I seem to remember Mr. Balanchine choreographed *Duo* in three or four days. The second and fourth movements have

very quick intricate steps, and with the help of our extraordinary pianist/conductor, Gordon Boelzner, Peter and I learned every note of that beautiful music backward and forward.

In the second movement of *Duo*, the first movement of dancing, Mr. Balanchine had Peter functioning as the big hand of a clock and I as the second hand. He also gave us a step and said our feet

Kay Mazzo and Peter Martins

Darci Kistler and Nikolaj Hübbe

were doing what the music was saying and our hands were conducting the music. In the fourth movement he had Peter playing the violin, which was me, in an arabesque and pulling me into a backward lunge in arabesque. Mr. Balanchine would show us a step and after seeing it danced, he would seem so happy with what he had created for Stravinsky.

Mr. Balanchine choreographed the last movement of the ballet the day before the premiere. Ronald Bates, our wonderful stage manager, and our crew worked so hard to try to block out all side lighting in the wings to make it pitch black onstage. Mr. Balanchine had not told Peter and me anything about the total darkness and we were both astonished about this concept and how the ballet would end.

I remember that after the ballet premiered, Lincoln Kirstein rushed backstage and kept saying Mr. Balanchine had created "a little jewel." Jerome Robbins also came backstage praising the ballet and congratulating Mr. Balanchine and all of us: Peter, Gordon, me, and our superb first violinist, Lamar Alsop. He then said to Mr. Balanchine, "George, tell me how you had the nerve to have no dance in the first movement. Didn't you think the audience might get bored?" Mr. Balanchine answered, "No, they have to first *hear* and understand and then *see* the beautiful music in my steps, which aren't so bad, dear."

After all the excitement of opening night, Mr. Balanchine came to me (and he was a man of few words of praise) and said, "Beautiful, beautiful dear," and I knew he felt Peter, Gordon, Lamar, and I had all honored Stravinsky and Mr. Balanchine's exquisite choreography. ❧

Kay Mazzo was born in Chicago, where she received early training before entering the Summer Course of the School of American Ballet at age twelve. She subsequently enrolled as a full-time student in SAB's advanced division in 1959. Following performances with Jerome Robbins' Ballets USA, Ms. Mazzo became a member of the New York City Ballet in 1961 and was promoted to principal dancer in 1968. In 1983, Ms. Mazzo joined the faculty of SAB, serving as a coordinator of curriculum between 1993 and 1997, and was appointed Co-Chairman of Faculty in October 1997.

Yvonne Borree and Peter Boal

New York City Ballet

Emeralds

Premiere: April 13, 1967
Company: New York City Ballet
Theater: New York State Theater, New York

By Mimi Paul

By Violette Verdy

When we started working on *Emeralds*, Balanchine said to me, "I want you to hear two pieces of music. Choose which you'd like to work to." This was an unexpected pleasure for me. I selected the ballade, and we immediately went to work on the variation.

This solo makes the dancer explore space. It used to be full of swirling, twisting movements and curved shapes. The challenge was to cover a large amount of space in a small amount of time, dancing with large, generous gestures. Throughout the years, much of the original solo was altered to suit other dancers. Although there are still wonderful moments

Continued on page 76

I met Mimi Paul when she was a very young student, and I was struck by her beautiful dancing even then—her charm, her mystery. So I was delighted when Mr. Balanchine decided to pair the two of us for the leading roles in *Emeralds*.

Emeralds is definitely one of Mr. B's most beautiful ballets. It represented his more romantic past from Europe. He was so completely marinated by France, so soaked in it. You recognize all the dramas, but there is no excess of feeling, of passions; everything has been distilled.

The ballet is full of that wonderful theme—Tchaikovsky's theme as a composer and Mr. Balanchine's theme so often as a choreographer—the longing, desiring, accepting, resignation, and letting go. And the resignation brings a wonderful lesson in quality of manners, of courtesy, and of selflessness. *Emeralds* is the most haunting section of *Jewels*, even though we can celebrate so much of Balanchine in the others too: St. Petersburg in *Diamonds*—an ode, an homage!

First I had a beginning section with Conrad Ludlow—searching, being resigned, and still

Continued on page 77

The cast of the New York City Ballet performs an ensemble

Mr. Balanchine rehearses Merrill Ashley

Continued from page 75

remaining within the choreography today, there were gems that unfortunately no longer exist.

The walking pas de deux I did with Francisco Moncion stands out for its originality. Just before we started working, Mr. B said to me, "I'm giving you something special to do." It was truly a treasured gift for me. The music evokes a dreamy, poetic feeling, which enveloped the two of us. The pas de deux is courtly and refined in manner, yet seamless in its unfolding.

It felt as if we were both in our own private world—an isolated, wondrous moment in time. 🙠

Mr. Balanchine rehearses Merrill Ashley and Gerald Ebitz

Mr. Balanchine during a rehearsal

Continued from page 75

looking for something and being caught by the man. There was beautiful intricate work in it, which has disappeared, but I still remember it, and I have it on tape. Parts of it disappeared because Mr. B got very annoyed with Robert Irving; he was going too fast in the last years of his conducting. Balanchine was always for speed but depending on when, and for what. Irving never changed, and Balanchine, really annoyed, decided to change the choreography because Irving was not going to change the tempo. So it was Balanchine himself doing the change, but it is a shame because there were things that were so gorgeous.

The solo is really the most extraordinary part. The mixture of syncopations and retards, the musical interpretation written right in the choreography, the changes of rhythms—amazing always. It has a sensuousness that is so French and a sense of discovery; it is an homage to a woman, definitely. The woman discovering the beauty of her own arms and reveling in her own body, making herself aware of it, so that she is pleasant and gracious with it, so that she can offer it and show it in a way that will please. The arms—offering them and taking them back, measuring her own riches, counting her own personal treasures, celebrating them, savoring them. The first time it is more of a private discovery and a private conversation with herself, a monologue. When it is repeated it becomes more an offering to others. At the end she retires into herself again.

Emeralds was full of longing, abandoning yourself to a man but knowing that you are still longing for something more. The man is wooing the woman; in the course of it she is caught up with him and goes along with him, but she is still longing for something else.

Later on, Mr. Balanchine created for me another pas de deux because he had that music in his pocket for years and years, and had not had time to use it when we did *Jewels* in 1967. I only danced that new section a few times before leaving the company in 1976 to direct the Paris Opera Ballet. ❧

New York City Ballet

Bonita Borne, Daniel Duell, Heather Watts

Of Swiss-Russian heritage, Mimi Paul was chosen by George Balanchine at age sixteen to be a recipient of a Ford Foundation scholarship to the School of American Ballet. Within six months she was invited to join the NYCB. Soon after that, her repertory as Principal Dancer included Symphony in C, Bugaku, Serenade, Apollo, Divertimento no.15, La Valse, and Liebeslieder Waltzes. Roles created for her included Emeralds, Valse Fantaisie, and Don Quixote. Ms. Paul also taught at the North Carolina School of the Arts for nine years and in 1997 staged Balanchine's Divertimento no. 15 in Italy. As a dancer, she was known for her superb sense of line, musicality, mysterious personality, and powerful stage presence resulting her own kind of magic in a variety of roles.

Violette Verdy danced more than 25 principal roles in a performance career that lasted from 1958 through 1976. In 1977, Miss Verdy became the first woman appointed Artistic Dancer of the Paris Opera Ballet; she served in that capacity until 1980 when she became co-Artistic Director of the Boston Ballet. In 1984, she returned to New York City Ballet, where she held the title of Teaching Associate. In addition to teaching at NYCB, Miss Verdy accepted teaching residencies and choreographic commissions at various institutions of higher education and at national and international dance companies. Since August of 1996, Miss Verdy has been a full-time Professor of Ballet at the School of Music at Indiana University, Bloomington, and contributes as Artistic Advisor for the Rock School of Ballet in Philadelphia, Pennsylvania.

Bonita Borne, Daniel Duell, Heather Watts

Karin von Aroldingen and Sean Lavery

Anton Korsakov of the Kirov Ballet poses for the camera

Wendy Whelan and Albert Evans

Episodes

PREMIERE: MAY 14, 1959
COMPANY: NEW YORK CITY BALLET
THEATER: CITY CENTER OF MUSIC AND DRAMA, NEW YORK

by Marian Horosko

They cringed when they saw the first rehearsal at the Graham studio for what was to be a collaborative effort between the New York City Ballet and the Martha Graham Contemporary Dance Company. Lincoln Kirstein and George Balanchine watched the Graham dancers crawling around on their knees and would have none of it for their dancers.

The conclusion was that Martha Graham would choreograph the first half of *Episodes* to Anton Webern's Passacaglia (op. 1) and Six Pieces for Orchestra (op. 6), and her company would dance the roles. Graham herself represented Mary Stuart, Queen of Scots, in a political endgame as a tennis match with Queen Elizabeth for which Mary lost her head. Heavily costumed by Karinska in Elizabethan garb, the Graham section included some of her principal dancers: Bertram Ross, Helen McGehee, Linda Hodes, Akiko Kanda, Gene McDonald, Ethel Winter, Richard Kuch, Dan Wagoner, and NYCB dancers Sallie Wilson and Ken Petersen as collaborative participants.

No Mozart or Tchaikovsky was heard at the first Balanchine rehearsal for *Episodes*, but rather the astringent, powerful, and reverential sound of Webern's Symphony (op. 21). Four couples using flexed feet, broken wrists, and lifts across the stage in quick battus became the new classicism of elegance and nobility.

A daringly sparse pas de deux to Five Pieces for Orchestra (op. 10) brought nervous titters from the audience, as they viewed functionless movement, passés turned in and upside-down splits overhead. The encounters were hesitant and fleeting but not

Peter Nauman and Karin von Aroldingen

Wendy Whelan and Albert Evans

Mr. Balanchine works with Karin von Aroldingen while Peter Nauman looks on

Mr. Balanchine works with Karin von Aroldingen while Peter Nauman looks on

without Balanchine's typical humor incorporated in tense relationships. Concerto (op. 24), another pas de deux plus four female dancers, found Balanchine's signature manipulation of entwining arms twisting branchlike with disturbing menace. There were no entrances or exits for the short movements—the dancers simply walked on or off for each section.

An unforgettable solo for Graham's Paul Taylor to Variations for Orchestra (op. 30) became a mesmerizing performance. Balanchine transformed the large, athletic size of the dancer and his ability to focus on small, simple movements into an emotional statement. Webern's majestic Ricercata for Six Voices from Bach's Musical Offering, with its eloquent formal fugue was visualized by Balanchine as a conclusion that expanded the modernism of his 1957 work, *Agon*. And at the finale, the dancers were kneeling, kneeling, kneeling in their black leotards, pink tights, and pointe shoes, looking more modern than the modern group.

After the opening May 14, 1959, subsequent performances dropped the first part and Taylor's solo. Although the ballet startled critics and audiences, it was well received. Four movements remain of Balanchine noble work. ෴

After leaving the New York City Ballet, Marian Horosko became an arts producer for TV and radio, created six dance seminars, authored five textbooks on ballet and modern dance, and is currently the New York correspondent for Dancer *magazine. She is listed in* Who's Who in America *and the* Oxford Dictionary of Dance *and is currently writing Graham dancer May O'Donnell's biography.*

Jukka Aromaa of the Finnish Ballet and Lourdes Lopez of the New York City Ballet

Lourdes Lopez and Erlends Zieminch

Firebird

PREMIERE: NOVEMBER 27, 1949
COMPANY: NEW YORK CITY BALLET
THEATER: CITY CENTER OF MUSIC AND DRAMA, NEW YORK

By Maria Tallchief

The final dress and lighting rehearsal for *Firebird* was scheduled for the morning of the premiere, and I arrived at the theater before dawn to be ready for the rehearsal at 7:00 A.M. A morning person, I did not mind starting work at that time. We desperately needed to rehearse.

A well-known classic, *Firebird* was Stravinsky's first great success. Michel Fokine choreographed it in 1910 and Tamara Karsavina danced the title role. For years the ballet was associated with Karsavina's name. Later, several versions were presented in America, including one at Ballet Theatre, in which Alicia Markova enjoyed a big success. Now George was choreographing a new production with me in the title role. Could I live up to these memorable interpretations?

Unbelievably, not only was this the first time my partner Francisco Moncion and I were dancing the ballet with the orchestra, it was the first time the production was lit. All that shone on me was a golden follow spot. When the music started to play, we began to dance. Surrounded by blackness, with brilliant spotlights blinding us, we found that the difficult parts now seemed impossible.

Nevertheless, the rehearsal was progressing smoothly. After the first arabesque, turning to face Frank and giving him my hand, I performed a glissade, a traveling step. Then after a preparation, while he continued moving, I went flying through space and threw myself into his arms. The force of my jump almost knocked him over. Somehow he managed to catch me, but he staggered from the shock. George had invented the movement; there seemed to be no balletic term to describe it adequately.

In the evening, once the ballet began, I stopped thinking about good or bad, success or failure, and just danced as well as I could. The variation was very difficult. But when Frank and I started the pas de deux, I felt secure. Standing upstage, I took an extra breath and then made the flying leap into his arms. Suddenly there I was being held by him upside down, my head practically touching the floor. An audible sigh rose in the audience. We heard it. It was as if they could not believe what they had seen.

One second before I had been at one end of the stage standing upright, yet now here I was at the other side suspended in Frank's arms. No one could see how it had been done. I must have flown.

This was one of the effects George had worked on so hard in rehearsal, and the way he had been able to create that moment was astonishing even to me. I had become this magical creature, the Firebird, yet I knew I had become the Firebird because George had made

Nina Fedorova and David Richardson

Jock Soto and Kathleen Tracey

Karin von Aroldingen and Peter Martins

me the Firebird. His genius had never been so clear to me as it was in that instant. When we finished the pas de deux the audience applauded so loudly that Frank and I were stunned. We had not expected it.

In fact, the audience seemed to be enjoying everything—the scene with the princesses and the monsters, the berceuse, and the final tableau, the wedding scene. In that scene, the music swelled to a glorious finish, but since there was no movement and all was still, it was as if there was a hush when the curtain fell. When it did, we all stood there in a state of shock. It was over! But calls had never been rehearsed, and nobody knew quite what to do.

The curtain rose again and as long as I live I will never forget the roar. A firestorm of applause erupted in the City Center, and the audience was on its feet clapping, stomping, and shouting. We just stood there, dumbfounded. People were screaming, "Bravo!" shouting themselves hoarse. It was pandemonium. The theater had turned itself into a football stadium, and the audience was in a frenzy.

When the curtain fell for the ninth or tenth time, they were still cheering. We were all in a daze. Then George took my arm to lead me out front for a bow. ❧

Maria Tallchief's autobiography Maria Tallchief: America's Prima Ballerina *was published in 1997 by Henry Holt. She received the Kennedy Center Honors in 1996.*

Lourdes Lopez and Erlends Zieminch

Jean-Pierre Bonnefoux, Susan Friedman, Victoria Hall, Linda Homek, Garielle Whittle

The Four Temperaments

PREMIERE: NOVEMBER 20, 1946
COMPANY: BALLET SOCIETY
THEATER: CENTRAL HIGH SCHOOL OF NEEDLE TRADES, NEW YORK

By Virginia Johnson

The piano begins: *da, da, dada.* I step out in answer, springing lightly into fifth position on pointe then circle my front leg to the back to finish in Mr. B's famous B+, hips forward, torso resting on the rhythm of syncopation. Across the stage, my partner invites me to dance. So begins the second temperament of the four, "Sanguinic." It was for me both a terror and delight to dance. The lilting, sprightly waltz choreographed to amuse was fun to dance and the mood of cheerful optimism the perfect foil for the technical demands.

Subtitled "A Dance Ballet Without Plot," the *Four Temperaments* is based on the ancient Greek notion that humans are made up of four different psychological and physical humors: melancholic, sanguinic, phlegmatic, and choleric. "An understanding of the Greek and medieval notion of the temperaments was merely the point of departure for both the composer and the choreographer," Balanchine wrote in his *101 Stories of the Great Ballets.* "Neither the music nor the ballet itself make special or literal interpretation of the idea."

By the time Dance Theater of Harlem added *Four T's* to its repertoire in 1979, the sets and costumes designed for the original production in 1946 had long been abandoned. The choreography had evolved as well. The broad outline of the ballet remained the same but the spare athleticism of the movement had been heightened so that the movement had taken on an archetypal feeling that matched even more the theme of expressing without interpreting the basic elements of human nature.

Dancing Balanchine always felt to me like putting on seven-league boots: Once you had them on you had to take those giant steps whether you were capable of them or not. The feeling was exhilarating. The challenge was cleanly and purely stated, but it was also daunting—failure was plainly evident.

"Sanguinic" offered a wry brilliance that did not come easily. Playful partnering, shifts in weight, multiple beats and those tricky turns made those few minutes onstage feel like dancing in a minefield. But then the reward: to circle the stage flying in my partner's arms as if from mountaintop to mountaintop and then to leap in exuberant triumph into the wings. ❧

New York City Ballet

Virginia Johnson is a former principal dancer with Dance Theatre of Harlem. She is currently the editor of Pointe *magazine.*

Dana Hanson and Sebastien Marcovici

Mr. Balanchine rehearses Merrill Ashley, Daniel Duell, and Elyse Borne while Rosemary Dunleavy and Merrill Brockway look on

Mr. Balanchine rehearses Renee Estopinal

Colleen Neary and Daniel Duell rehearse as Mr. Balanchine looks on

Mr. Balanchine rehearses David Richardson and Renee Estopinal

Adam Lüders, Nina Fedorova, Maria Calegari, Garielle Whittle, Linda Homek

David Richardson gets a lesson from Mr. Balanchine

Merrill Ashley and Daniel Duell

Merrill Ashley and Daniel Duell

Peter Boal (center) flanked by two New York City Ballet dancers

Ethan Stiefel

Harlequinade

PREMIERE: FEBRUARY 4, 1965
COMPANY: NEW YORK CITY BALLET
THEATER: NEW YORK STATE THEATER, NEW YORK

by Suki Schorer

Balanchine choreographed *Harlequinade* less than a year after the company moved to the New York State Theater. It was a two-act story ballet by Marius Petipa that he had done at the Maryinsky as a child, and he used the original score (by Riccardo Drigo), although not all the original music, at least not in the first version of the ballet. Balanchine not only followed the libretto, he kept all the mime; he would go over to the piano, look at the score, read what it said, and translate the French.

He used to singsong the mime to us. I can still hear his voice rehearsing my first variation: "You have an idea! Run and get the key. Show him the key, no, no. Taunt him with the key. Now run and do arabesque. He reaches for the key; you penchée and take it away." The "he" was Deni Lamont, who played the role of Pierrot. I was his wife, Pierrette.

Balanchine had a genius for casting. Could anyone have found a better Harlequin than Eddie [Edward Villella]? Or a better Columbine than Patty [Patricia McBride]? Patty's second-act variation, the berceuse, was slow and dreamy; her presence filled the music—her eyes, her port de bras, her whole body. There was an "oriental" step in which she talked with her eyes and made hand gestures like lotus blossoms; it was a little like *Bugaku*. And when she blew her final kisses, you felt she was sending them straight to your heart.

Balanchine knew me like a book. He knew I had an older brother and that I liked to tease him, and he used that knowledge in rehearsing the mime. And how well he knew me as a dancer. My variation was full of hops and jumps on pointe, steps I loved to do, perky and full of zip, just like my personality. I remember Carol Sumner, the lead Alouette, skimming the floor, as light as a bird.

Students of the School of American Ballet

Ethan Stiefel

Harlequinade was a big ballet, with real sets and commedia dell'arte costumes by Rouben Ter-Arutunian. When the ballet started, I was inside the house with Patty. I was never sure when to open the balcony door to spy on Pierrot. (I was supposed to steal the key from him to unlock the house so Patty could meet Eddie.) "Oh," she'd say, "it's on the pretty music." One day we got to talking, and we missed the pretty music. So I never stepped out on the balcony; I just flew down the stairs and started my variation. Hugo Fiorato, who was conducting, came back after the first act and congratulated me. "You danced so well, Suki." "Hugo," I said, "I missed my first entrance. You must have been busy conducting."

Balanchine never said anything to me about the ballet. But I think he must have been excited by the size of the stage, which enabled him to do the big story ballets he had seen as a child. And who knows, maybe the relatively intimate

Mr. Balanchine and Rosemary Dunleavy rehearse students of the School of American Ballet

Harlequinade was a rehearsal for the grand-scaled *Don Quixote,* the story ballet of his life, which he choreographed just after *Harlequinade.*

In 1968 Balanchine added the Carnival number to the ballet, and in 1973 a dance for twenty-four children using the complete score, as Petipa had done. The story was the same, but I always felt that our version—the original one—was more compact, with a poetry of its own. 🖎

Suki Schorer joined the New York City Ballet in 1959, achieving the rank of Principal Dancer in 1968. Soon after she joined, Balanchine asked her to teach part time and in 1972 made her the first NYCB dancer to teach full time at SAB. She regularly lectures on Balanchine aesthetics, guest teaches in the United States and abroad, and is the author of Suki Schorer on Balanchine Technique.

Ethan Stiefel

Mr. Balanchine rehearses Mikhail Baryshnikov

Kyra Nichols, Sean Lavery, Leonid Koslov, Suzanne Farrell, Patricia McBride, Ib Andersen, Bart Cook, Stephanie Saland

Liebeslieder Walzer

PREMIERE: NOVEMBER 22, 1960
COMPANY: NEW YORK CITY BALLET
THEATER: CITY CENTER OF MUSIC AND DRAMA, NEW YORK

by Karin von Aroldingen

Ever since my early childhood, waltzing was my favorite way of moving. It elevated my spirits. The wonderful waltzing tunes always served to put me in a good mood. Balanchine once said that "it was like rocking on a gondola."

When I joined the New York City Ballet, I saw and worked on so many wonderful ballets of Balanchine's in so many different styles. Of course, when I saw the fairly new choreography of Brahms's *Liebeslieder Walzer,* I was transformed by the graceful dancing and the various loving moods of gallantry and capriciousness. I wanted to run onstage and join the dancers. *Liebeslieder* is sung in German in four voices. As a viewer, one does not have to understand the old German poetry and Balanchine did not intend to dance to the words, but to the sounds of the voices, again expressing the mood of the music and the sound. Four hands, two piano players, cue the singer and dancers. The dancers, four couples, visualize the harmonic sequences of so many characteristics. Waltzes like the Ländler (a peasant dance that became the classic waltz); a jota with Spanish accents; the long, slow, smooth waltzes in pas de deux, pas de trois, and pas de quatre. More than an hour of just waltzing, but what variety. Brahms wrote the music in two parts—the first takes place in an imaginary ballroom or private drawing room. In the second part, the women change costumes and replace the little satin heel shoes with toe shoes. The elevation and imagery of the sound for the dancers is like being in a dreamlike world.

Suzanne Farrell, whom I understudied, left the company for some time. I could not believe my luck! I cannot describe in words what it meant to dance her part. To watch it from the other side is absolutely stunning, but to dance it—to me it was a step closer to happiness.

In 1976 Mr. Balanchine told me to go to Vienna to stage *Liebeslieder Walzer* for the Vienna State Opera Ballet's upcoming season. At the time I was dancing alot with New York City Ballet—what did Mr. B mean to make me stop dancing now? All I could bring myself to say was, "I can't do this." "Yes, dear," he said, "you have a body to show (certainly waltzing), eyes to see, and besides you speak a little German." Well, I studied for months and months. Sometimes I would "borrow" a dancer and teach the girl's part while I did the male partnering. In three weeks of staging, I barely made it. When Mr. Balanchine arrived I was a nervous wreck. He remarked, "Not bad, dear," a big compliment from him. He gave the ballet the finishing touches and I loved it. ❧

Maria Kowroski

Ib Andersen, Stephanie Saland, Kyra Nichols, Joseph Duell, Suzanne Farrell, Sean Lavery

Patricia McBride and Bart Cook

Stephanie Saland and Ib Andersen

Suzanne Farrell

A Midsummer Night's Dream

Premiere: January 17, 1962
Company: New York City Ballet
Theater: City Center of Music and Drama, New York

By Francia Russell

Balanchine often said his inspiration for *A Midsummer Night's Dream* came from Mendelssohn's music more than from Shakespeare's play. Because music was always the source of his creative energy, one can hardly question this statement. However, the ballet's fidelity to the text and its perfect translation of the characters' words and motivation into movement and mime reveal an intimate familiarity with Shakespeare's radiant poetry.

Teaching *Midsummer* to a group of dancers is pure joy. Oberon, Titania, Puck, Bottom, and the four lovers are each delineated in exquisite detail by the choreography and in no need of speech to convey every nuance of their roles. Since each movement in the ballet is a reflection of both the play and the score, timing is the most critical element. The wit, charm, and satire are only realized if perfectly timed and, therefore, apparently spontaneous.

As ravishing as is the choreography for the principal characters, some of the most magical moments in the ballet belong to the children: the end of the overture where the bugs and fairies comfort Helena and then settle into a puddle of small, sleepy bodies as the butterflies bourrée sweetly across the stage; the earnestness and fleeting patterns of the small dancers with Oberon in the Scherzo; and the children's return at the end of the ballet as they reclaim the fairy kingdom and bid the audience farewell with twinkling fireflies.

Some critics saw Balanchine himself in Puck. In rehearsals he was equally convincing as Oberon, Titania, Bottom, and any of the other characters. But there is no doubt his childhood memories of performing as a bug in a staging of the play in St. Petersburg shaped the delight of what Lincoln Kirstein called his "wholly unsentimental deployment of small fairies."

New York City Ballet

Mikhail Baryshnikov

The second act, Divertissement, is the meeting of only two creative sensibilities. In the fourteen-year-old Mendelssohn's String Symphony, Mr. Balanchine found the ideal platform for a choreographic portrait of the highest pinnacle of love. This pas de deux of porcelain clarity stands in stark contrast to the shenanigans of the principal characters of Act I and highlights their foolishness as the story is being brought to a happy conclusion.

Not universally well received, *A Midsummer Night's Dream* was the first original full-length ballet created in the United States. Forty years later, it remains the most magical and in another hundred years it may

Mikhail Baryshnikov and Jean-Pierre Frohlich

Kyra Nichols and Philip Neal

increase in appeal even more. Balanchine's fascination with choreographic structure and with revealing the human body at work belied the fact that when he wanted to tell a story with charm, color, psychological insight, and theatricality, he was the master. Nowhere is this clearer than in this delicate masterpiece uniting reverence for Shakespeare's poetry and Mendelssohn's music with his muse, the art of dance. ❧

Francia Russell was a soloist and ballet mistress with the New York City Ballet. She is now Co-Artistic Director of the Pacific Northwest Ballet and Director of the PNB School.

New York City Ballet

Karin von Aroldingen

Helgi Tomasson

Jennifer Fournier and Runqiao Du of the Suzanne Farrell Ballet

Monumentum pro Gesualdo and Movements for Piano and Orchestra

PREMIERE: APRIL 9, 1963 AND NOVEMBER 16, 1960
COMPANY: NEW YORK CITY BALLET
THEATER: CITY CENTER OF MUSIC AND DRAMA, NEW YORK

by Mindy Aloff

Movements for Piano and Orchestra was the first Balanchine ballet I ever saw live. The performance was around 1964, at City Center. I seem to remember that *A Midsummer Night's Dream* was also on the bill, although that programming would be quite unusual. The leads in *Movements* were the teenage Suzanne Farrell, just a couple of years older than I was, and Jacques d'Amboise. I was sitting in the first row of the mezzanine, very close to the action, and I could not get over the deluxe power of Farrell's legs, which she operated as fluently and with as much accuracy as if they were arms. There was also a certain strangeness in her deportment: she did not seem to will her dancing; instead, her body was a kind of conduit for impulses that originated in some offstage generator. (Stravinsky wanted to call the ballet *Electric Currents*.)

The landscape of the whole work had a look of unconscious process: the sharp transitions between phrases, so that nothing counted as a linking step—everything was pure subject; the radical reproportioning of scale from one step or gesture to another, sometimes on a single count; the dreamlike arboretum of images made by the chamber-sized corps of six women; the eloquent yet untranslatable language of the formations for the principals. The dancers really did seem to be another species from the puzzled youngster trying to parse their austere choreography—no running, no sustained jumping, and, it seemed, no repeats.

Even more difficult to absorb was the music, much of which consisted of silence where the meter and pulse could only be felt. That Zen-like calm of execution against the spooky, anxious figures being executed and that apsychological, creaturely look is what I have come to associate with Balanchine's "Just do the steps." Indeed, they have remained a standard for me of what "modernism" means in theatrical dancing. (It was not so different, either, from the look of Merce Cunningham's *RainForest,* which I first saw a few years later.)

I have never seen a more intellectually absorbing ballet, not even by Balanchine. Watching Farrell painstakingly analyze the principal roles last fall for the Balanchine Foundation did not in any way demystify their essential paradox: the pas de deux make a great, sweeping statement out of exactly tessellated, surgically measured-off modules of speech.

Movements for Piano and Orchestra was given its premiere in the spring of 1963, the same season as the premiere of *Bugaku,* another experiment with classical

Darci Kistler and Nilas Martins

Eva Natanya, Riolama Lorenzo, Dana Hanson

Mindy Aloff's writing on theatrical dance and other arts has appeared in Chronicle of Higher Education, New Republic, The New York Times, The New Yorker, *and many other periodicals and anthologies. She is a consultant to The George Balanchine Foundation and an adjunct lecturer in dance history and criticism at Barnard College.*

syntax and vocabulary. *Monumentum pro Gesualdo* was first danced in the fall of 1960, one week before the premiere of *Liebeslieder Walzer*. Since the mid-1960s, *Movements* and *Monumentum* have been performed together. Farrell, herself, would dance the leads in both, as Diana Adams—who did perform *Monumentum* (which was made on her) and for whom *Movements* was also intended—would probably have danced both.

I first saw *Monumentum* in the early 1980s, when Farrell was dancing it. Chivalric in its manners, preindustrial—even medieval—in its imagery, set to three Renaissance madrigals (by Gesualdo, Prince of Venosa) whose songlike character lingers in Stravinsky's bracing arrangement for instruments, this exquisite ballet seems to have been hewn from stone. *Monumentum*, so reverent in its images of the ballerina, can feel merely devotional in a lax performance. Yet, although the steps per se are not experimental, their frosty, spellbinding grace is, in emotional terms, quite cutting edge. ❧

Suzanne Farrell and Sean Lavery

Helene Alexopoulos and Charles Askegaard

Ib Andersen (left) and Damian Woetzel (right) each as the male lead in Mozartiana

Mozartiana

Premiere: June 4, 1981
Company: New York City Ballet
Theater: Tchaikovsky Festival at the New York State Theater, New York

By Ib Andersen

To me, *Mozartiana* is about art, and maybe about artists. It is also about Mozart, through Tchaikovsky, and about Balanchine at that stage of his life, about the artist at the end of his life, when everything comes together and you are able to pare everything down to its essence. This ballet is so distilled.

I think it is a conversation, my role and Suzanne's. I always felt that Suzanne and I were talking to each other while we were dancing, that we were saying, "I think this," "Oh! You think that?" but it was never between a man and a woman. It was between two artists having a conversation that is enriching, inspirational, and very enjoyable. It is as though you are talking with someone with whom you are on the same wavelength. You are thinking the same things, but you are each articulating your thoughts in a different way, and after the conversation is over, you are emotionally and mentally high.

[Balanchine] did not say any of this, of course. He gave the steps, and if you are sensitive enough, between the steps and the music, it is right there in front of your nose. Of course, it is different from person to person, but that is what was great about Balanchine. In almost all his ballets, you can do it in many different ways, but probably the truest way of doing it is to be yourself. You have to understand, totally, what the ballet is about. But in the end, you have to be yourself.

When he was creating the ballet, it was during the Tchaikovsky Festival, and there were a lot of different people doing new ballets. Balanchine, as always, gave himself the least amount of time. He gave everyone else as much time as they wanted, but we started quite

late; he did the ballet in no more than two weeks, right before the premiere.

To be quite honest, on opening night I do not think we were ready to do it. We had not worked enough. We basically just had learned the steps. It had not molded into our bodies, and we had not

taken it to the place where it later went because it was so new.

Later on when we did it, it became a little bit of a cult ballet because it was the newest and the latest Balanchine, and everyone was coming to see it. There was such a special atmosphere about this ballet.

Suzanne Farrell and Ib Andersen

Mr. Balanchine rehearses

It was such a privilege. [Suzanne and I] both felt that dancing *Mozartiana* was almost a religious experience. I think everyone involved in that ballet knew that it was special, very special, and that we should feel lucky that we were in it. There was a kind of concentration in the wings when we were waiting to go on; I do not remember other ballets having quite that intensity. And it would be the same for people who would watch it from the wings. *Mozartiana* has tremendous respect from ballet dancers. ❧

Born in 1954 in Copenhagen, Ib Andersen was exposed to dance from an early age. At age seven, he was accepted into the School of the Royal Danish Ballet and was asked to join the Ballet at the age of sixteen. By the age of twenty, Mr. Andersen was a Principal Dancer for the Royal Danish Ballet; soon after he accepted an invitation by Mr. Balanchine to join the New York City Ballet. Throughout his years at the NYCB, Mr. Andersen had several principal roles created for him, including those in *Ballade, Mozartiana,* and *Davidsbundlertanzer.* After retiring from NYCB in 1990, Mr. Andersen traveled the world staging Balanchine ballets and choreographing new works. He now serves as the Artistic Director for Ballet Arizona.

Nikolaj Hübbe

Mr. Balanchine rehearses Suzanne Farrell and Ib Andersen

Suzanne Farrell and students of the School of American Ballet

Paloma Herrera of American Ballet Theatre

The Nutcracker

PREMIERE: FEBRUARY 2, 1954
COMPANY: NEW YORK CITY BALLET
THEATER: CITY CENTER OF MUSIC AND DRAMA, NEW YORK

By Ellen Switzer

The original *Nutcracker* was commissioned by the Russian Court in the nineteenth century. The music was composed by Tchaikovsky, and the choreography was supposed to have come from Marius Petipa, the senior ballet master of the Russian Imperial Ballet; however, Petipa got very sick, and his assistant, Lev Ivanov, finally choreographed the ballet. Depending on which dance history you read, it was either a moderate success or a downright flop.

The story of the ballet is based on a fairy tale written by E. T. A. Hoffman, a well-known German writer who was a pessimistic, gloomy person, generally unimpressed with humanity. On the whole, he seemed to be a very unsuitable writer to produce a child's fairy tale. So, it's no wonder that most versions that are still danced today look as if someone was not entirely sure what the story was supposed to mean. Now there are dozens of other *Nutcrackers*—many with adults playing children. None of them work very well since an adult pretending to be a child tends to look childish rather than childlike.

When he was a child in Russia, George Balanchine danced the Nutcracker Prince in the Ivanov ballet. In 1954 he decided to choreograph his

Miranda Weese

Scene from The Nutcracker *with students from the School of American Ballet*

Christopher Wheeldon

own version based on the Russian *Nutcracker*. Balanchine knew that the gloomy story would not work with American children. Also, he did not seem to like it much himself. So the Balanchine *Nutcracker* is warm and happy, with family members who love and respect each other.

Some of the other *Nutcrackers* in which adults danced the principal roles ended with the separation of the Nutcracker Prince and Marie and, therefore, usually seem to strike a melancholic note.

Balanchine's *Nutcracker* is similar to the Russian version, but the characters he created are more human, friendly, and warm. There is no villain. Even Drosselmeier is mysterious rather than truly frightening. The family is close and happy. Everyone, including the grandparents, is treated with the greatest respect by the choreographer.

The story is simple and direct. The Stahlbaums are having a huge Christmas party. Their children, Marie and Fritz, have not yet seen the Christmas tree and are waiting for the guests to arrive. Marie decides to look through the keyhole to see what is going on. She and her little brother are fascinated with the Christmas decorations.

After the guests arrive, the festivities really get started. After everyone has arrived, and the gifts have been exchanged, a mysterious visitor called Drosselmeier enters with his nephew. His Christmas gift for Marie is a huge nutcracker. It is obvious that Marie likes the gift better than anything else she has received. Her little brother, Fritz, is furious and jealous and tries to snatch the nutcracker away from his sister. In the process, he breaks it. Marie is disconsolate. Drosselmeier tries to comfort her and repairs the nutcracker using his big, white handkerchief as a bandage. Marie stops weeping and holds the nutcracker close in her arms. By then, the time has come for the party to end. All the guests get their coats and go home. Marie and Fritz are told to go to bed.

Marie decides to return to the parlor to look at the Christmas tree again; however, she is very tired and goes to sleep on the couch. Her mother finds her and puts her own warm shawl over her.

As the clock strikes twelve, Drosselmeier reappears sitting on top of a grandfather clock. Suddenly a flock of mice with their ruler, the Mouse King, appear. Marie wakes and is shocked and frightened. She looks for help. The nutcracker changes into a handsome young prince who with his sword tries to chase all the mice away and protect Marie. The Mouse King is startled and turns around to look at Marie and possibly attack her. Far from being afraid, Marie takes off her slipper and tosses it at the Mouse King's head. He is distracted enough so that the Nutcracker Prince can get to him and kill him. At that point, all the mice flee, and the Prince and Marie are left along together. He opens the French doors, and he and Marie walk out into the snow. The Prince has taken the Mouse King's crown and puts it on Marie's head, and off they go into the Land of Sweets. That ends the first act.

In the second act the children are in the Land of the Sweets, where they are greeted by the Sugar Plum Fairy. The Prince tells her in pantomime the story of how he and Marie escaped the danger of the mice. She is very impressed with the loyalty and bravery of the children and invites them to stay for a party. They are led to a special throne—a place of honor—where they are served delicious food and are able to watch the many dances to be performed by the citizens of the Land of the Sweets.

Unfortunately, even the most wonderful party must come to an end. Special transportation has been arranged for the guests of honor. A sleigh pulled by reindeer arrives. The Sugar Plum Fairy bids the children good-bye, and, while the citizens of the Land of the Sweets wave and cheer, Marie and the Prince ride high into the sky away from the magic country to their home. ❧

Jerome Robbins

Ethan Stiefel

Isabelle Guerin of the Paris Opera Ballet and Damian Woetzel of the New York City Ballet

Mr. Balanchine rehearses

Children of the School of American Ballet

Svetlana Zaharova of the Kirov Ballet

Stephanie Saland, Sandra Jennings, Kyra Nichols, Merrill Ashley, Christopher d'Amboise

Ellen Switzer is a journalist who has written regularly for a number of women's magazines including Vogue, Glamour, Self, *and* Family Circle. *She has also written several books, including* Dancers! Horizons in American Dance, *and* Nutcracker (A Story and A Ballet). *Both books were illustrated with photographs by Costas. In recent years, dance has been one of her primary interests, espeically the choreographies of George Balanchine.*

Benjamin Bowman

Heather Watts

Nilas Martins

Orpheus

PREMIERE: APRIL 28, 1948
COMPANY: BALLET SOCIETY
THEATER: CITY CENTER OF MUSIC AND DRAMA, NEW YORK

By Don Daniels

As a ballet about an ancient legend, the Balanchine-Stravinsky *Orpheus* has become something of a legend itself, especially since the move of New York City Ballet to Lincoln Center where the State Theater stage is too large for the redesigned Isamu Noguchi décor and the intimacy of the mimetic action. Despite its ravishing musical score, the ballet's revivals have not been frequent, and this prevents NYCB from representing its evening-length "Stravinsky Trilogy" consisting of *Apollo*, *Orpheus*, and *Agon*. *Orpheus* is famous for a number of reasons. Balanchine and Stravinsky worked closely on its planning and realization. On seeing the finished work, Morton Baum invited Balanchine's and Lincoln Kirstein's Ballet Society to become a constituent of City Center, thus bringing into being the New York City Ballet and giving it a stage for regular seasons. Subsequently the Noguchi lyre designed for *Orpheus* became a company symbol. A series of George Platt Lynes photographs, supervised in the studio by Balanchine himself, provided a record of the glamorous first cast.

The ballet is unique for its theme and style. Balanchine and Stravinsky were able to address the career of the artist—here the master-musician—against a pre-Classical background of Eros and Thanatos. The ballet's immediate American audience knew something about suburban provisions for reproduction and dying; perhaps in that sense—a professional class's twentieth-century retreat from city living—the ballet touched a contemporary nerve. The ritual action is accomplished primarily in mime or dance-mime. Edwin Denby commented after the premiere on the sense of temporal dilation through much of the ballet, and achieved timelessness that

allowed Eurydice's preemptory seduction of Orpheus's gaze and the Bacchnantes' attack a deliberate and obscene fatality. (The Orpheus myth is presented as offering primarily pagan forms of consolation.) Balanchine's staging made references to Martha Graham (especially through the Noguchi connection) and to Fred Astaire (Maria Tallchief, the original Eurydice, has pointed to jazzy accents in her solo).

Mr. Balanchine rehearses Kay Mazzo and Mikhail Baryshnikov

The source is pastoral, and the underlying point of view is that of allusive, sophisticated urban artists.

Orpheus is one of Balanchine' ostentatiously syncretic works. He and Stravinsky decided early to use an Angel of Death to guide their *Orpheus* into the underworld, a figure (Francisco Moncion in the first cast) that relates back to Balanchine's female Dark

Mr. Balanchine rehearses Mikhail Baryshnikov

Angel in *Serenade.* The explanation was that Neoplatonic uses of Orphic beliefs had added angels to the legend in subsequent retellings. But the Death figure also allowed a Hermes-like psychopomp (Hermes was not only the inventor of the lyre but a conductor of souls to Hades). Thus the Angel of Death was theatrical machinery for visualizing the poet-musician's blinding, inspiration, and final abandonment. Throughout the ballet, Balanchine's fantasy flows. Archaic effects are achieved with the simplest of means. For example, in his opening solo before Eurydice's *stela*, Orpheus briefly balances his lyre against the stage with his chin, an almost tactile image of mute funerary tribute. The Angel thereafter turns a memento of Eurydice into the mask that blinds Orphus, who will relinquish it only when a Bacchante tears it from his grasp. When the Angel oversees Orpheus's concert for the Plutonian court, the musician empties himself of melody and then kneels in passivity before Death, his body bowed into the shape of an Orphic egg, forehead to earth. Such "primitive" stage imageries evoke the piercing suggestiveness of ancient verse, like the famous Orphic metaphor, "A kid I have fallen into milk." They connect the work to a range of experience that feels truly pagan.

Mr. Balanchine rehearses

Contemporary reports from the early performances characterize Tallchief's Eurydice as both vulnerable and ravenous. Francisco Moncion continued to perform the role of the Angel of Death well into the 1970s. He was able to convey an ominous, insinuating control over the action (and over the blinded Orpheus) while remaining "not there" in the tradition of the Oriental stage manager. Nicholas Magallanes as Orpheus was required to hold the eye throughout the performance, and he did so with a mode of dance-mime that Balanchine almost single-handedly brought into the mid-twentieth century. (Balanchine claimed that his Maryinsky teacher Samuil Konstantinovich Andrianov had impressed him early with how to represent a poetic figure in ballet mime.) It is a lyric style now nearly vanished from our stages. For those lucky enough to have watched Balanchine himself rehearse his ballets and demonstrate their actions to his dancers, *Orpheus* contains many ghost-images of the ballet master: here is how a poet, a musician, a dancer receives the blows of fate. This is how he moves. ❧

Don Daniels is Associate Editor of Ballet Review. *He lives in New York City and has been writing on dance in* Ballet Review *and other publications since 1972.*

Mr. Balanchine rehearses Mikhail Baryshnikov

Mr. Balanchine rehearses Mikhail Baryshnikov

Mr. Balanchine rehearses Mikhail Baryshnikov

Mikhail Baryshnikov and New York City Ballet

Prodigal Son

PREMIERE: FEBRUARY 23, 1950
COMPANY: NEW YORK CITY BALLET
THEATER: CITY CENTER OF MUSIC AND DRAMA, NEW YORK

By Edward Villella

It is a marvelous ballet and a fabulous role to dance.

Every artist attempts to portray his or her role the way it was originally intended. With a Balanchine ballet, that takes a lot of understanding and investigation because Balanchine was not fond of getting into verbal intellectualisms. His favorite phraseology was, "Don't talk, just do it." He knew us so well, and he knew what it was that he wanted so well, that he simply moved us and guided us.

It took me quite a while—and a couple of hints from him—to understand the origins of the style, the history, where things came from. Balanchine was fond of not saying anything, but he was also fond of coming backstage after a performance and dropping one or two little words. For example, there was a gesture that I was struggling with in the opening of the pas de deux. I just did not have it. He finally said to me, "Byzantine icons, dear. Byzantine icons." Every bit of the port de bras was from those icons, and that opened up the world for me to begin to investigate the role further.

I was twenty, and had not been educated in the world of ballet; I had gone to military school. But I had instincts, I had ears, and I had eyes. I watched Balanchine, and he spoke to us with his body. That also was a process for me, to listen to what he was saying with his body. I think he did not want us to eat up the scenery and overdo.

I had no sense of mime. I joined the New York City Ballet in 1957, the year of *Agon*. And here was a title role, a story role, and something very, very easy to inflate. But I would get little indications from him. For example, during the lift where the Siren sits on his neck, he goes down between her legs and puts her up on his shoulder. Balanchine said, "No, no, no. Don't rush it, because she's going to be up there smoking a cigarette." And you immediately got a sense of these early cigarette posters. Every time he said something, it always lent itself to the subject, and if you listened and tried to analyze it, you got closer to the essence of what he was trying to do.

Today, when I coach, I prefer to let the dancers know what I know. I prefer to let them know what I

Karin von Aroldingen

Karin von Aroldingen and Mikhail Baryshnikov

Mr. Balanchine rehearses Mikhail Baryshnikov

heard, what I saw, why I approach something in this manner and fashion, and then break it down for them. This is a process. It is developing a characterization, an essence of a period and a style, and it is not all about technique and your individual sense of yourself, your ego. That is a hard thing to do. You learn by teaching and you learn by doing. So many things came to me during the performance, and that is the awareness that I have to provide for these people—because, left on their own, they will basically chew it up.

I have learned, of course, from coaching the ballet. It is an ongoing experience. When you rehearse a ballet like this, there is the wonder of being in the presence of the mind of Balanchine. When we are rehearsing, we are indeed in the presence of the mind of that man. ꙮ

Mr. Balanchine rehearses Mikhail Baryshnikov

Mr. Balanchine rehearses Mikhail Baryshnikov and Shaun O'Brien

A former Principal Dancer for the New York City Ballet, Edward Villella is recognized nationally and internationally for his contributions to the field of classical dance and arts education. He originated many roles in the NYCB repertory, perhaps the most famous of which is the 1960 revival of Balanchine's Prodigal Son. Mr. Villella is a former producer/director for the PBS series Dance in America, and in 1975 he won an Emmy Award for his CBS television production of Harlequinade. In recognition of his achievements, President Clinton presented to Mr. Villella the 1997 National Medal of Arts. Also in 1997, Mr. Villella was named a Kennedy Center Honoree, and was inducted into the Florida Artists Hall of Fame. Since 1985 he has served as the Founding Artistic Director of Miami City Ballet.

Mikhail Baryshnikov performs solo in Prodigal Son

Mikhail Baryshnikov performs solo in Prodigal Son

Mikhail Baryshnikov performs solo in Prodigal Son

Mikhail Baryshnikov

Mikhail Baryshnikov

Mikhail Baryshnikov

Nicole Hlinka

Raymonda Variations

PREMIERE: DECEMBER 7, 1961
COMPANY: NEW YORK CITY BALLET
THEATER: CITY CENTER OF MUSIC AND DRAMA

By Andris Liepa

When Nina [Ananiashvili] and I arrived in New York in 1988 with the Bolshoi Tour, I asked the organizer of the tour to help us get some work with the New York City Ballet. She was very receptive to the idea and spoke with people in the NYCB. By January we received an invitation to come to the New York City Ballet as guest performers.

At that time I was in love with *Apollo* and with a Jerry Robbins piece, *Afternoon of a Faun*. And I thought it would be very easy for us to start with these two ballets. But *Apollo* was not in the repertory at that time. And I don't know why we were not doing the Jerry Robbins piece, but I think Peter [Martins] decided that we should start with some works from the New York City Ballet created by Mr. Balanchine. And I think he chose *Raymonda* because we had already done that piece, it was in the repertory, and we were very familiar with the music.

My first couple of rehearsals were with Peter, but he had a lot on his plate because he was also preparing the Balanchine Festival. So, since Peter had less time to rehearse, we began to rehearse with Adam Lüders, who was preparing to become a teacher. And it was really, really, hard work for us because of the increased tempos, and the pressure that we had at that time was extremely powerful. It was supposed to be easy for us because we knew the music and had only to learn new choreography, but it was more difficult for us than to work on *Symphony in C*.

I'm sure Mr. B had seen the original Grigorovich version, the classical version, and I had seen a couple of steps from that version, but Mr. B was trying to get away from the original version and to find his own

hearing of the music. I love the variations. They were completely different. And he staged the symphonic music. He was hearing what Mr. Glazounov was writing. I wouldn't say it was strange. It was not what we were used to, but I loved it.

It was difficult because my variations were extremely fast compared with the tempo we were used to dancing in Russia. I am still very familiar with the music. As I said before, Mr. B was creating a new variation, with the same music but twice as fast. Rudolf [Nureyev], who was taking classes at the NYCB, came to some early rehearsals and made a couple of very interesting suggestions to help me make the transition from the Russian school of ballet to the American school of ballet.

When you know a ballet, the tempo is inside of you, and the choreography as well. I probably knew a couple of steps from the variation in *Raymonda,* but they were in completely different places in terms of the action. I think probably the most difficult part for us in performing this piece was that we already knew the music and the choreography, but we had to relearn everything in a new way.

The New York City Ballet was an incredible school. The costume I used was memorable, because it was the costume that Peter Martins had used for his *Tchaikovsky Pas [de Deux]*. It was a great costume, and I loved it very much. (In fact, Peter Martins said that we might take these costumes back to Russia and I later gave the costume to [Igor Zelensky], who is still dancing in it. Traditions, they never die. They go from one dancer to another.) All the details that were used in this production were very important. [Nina and I]

Peter Schaufuss

lived in the apartment of Marianna Tcherkassky, and there were video machines there so we had a chance to learn everything and rehearse in the apartment, which was very beautiful and located next to the Metropolitan and the New York City Ballet. Besides the actual rehearsing in the theater, we had a chance to rehearse all the pieces at home as well.

Opening night went well, but it was incredibly difficult to show our power in this ballet the first night. We were shaking because it was another stage, another tempo, another choreography, and nerves. We used to do some incredible things in the Bolshoi, and it was very difficult to prove we could do the same things in Balanchine's style. The second performance was much easier for us because we were more used to the tempos, the company, and everything else.

Usually the American style of working on stage is that the first twenty performances or so are outside of New York City. So by the time the performers get to New York City, they're used to the number of people in the audience and are showing their best abilities after they have toured around America. This is what we were missing in terms of inventing ourselves in New York. But it didn't take away from the greatness of the moment.

Today, it is not unusual for Russian dancers to get contracts from the New York City Ballet. But before, that wasn't possible. Soviet dancers had to get official

Miranda Weese and Peter Boal

Violette Verdy and Peter Schaufuss

permission from the Soviet government to go and learn things in the Balanchine company. And we had just one month to learn everything.

I didn't feel that people disliked me; they were very interested in everything we were doing. I have great admiration for Peter Martins and what he did for us. He was the director. The major decisions weren't just his, but he gave a chance to us to do it. And I know that he was proud that we worked very hard. It wasn't the easiest work, but it was a success because he gave us the chance. The audience loved the experiment. I think it was the best example of how we could work after that.

After our tour and our return to Russia, we noticed a lot of changes in the way we danced. Everybody was saying to me, "You do things much faster than you did before." Even the steps I was doing before, they were much slower, and much more powerful, but we got the easiness and lightness that the New York City Ballet has, that Mr. Balanchine taught them. Nina and I became different dancers by working in America. Everything that we're doing now is a result of our working with the New York City Ballet during those one and a half months. It changed our lives. Nina now regularly comes to rehearse and dance in New York and dancers like Igor Zelensky have a chance to work in New York for a couple of years. But we were the first. I think our collaboration totally changed the opinion of the New York City Ballet toward Russian dancers. Step by step, we created a new era for Russian ballet in America. ❧

After eight years with the Bolshoi Ballet, Andris Liepa (with partner Nina Ananiashvili) became the first Russian dancer to receive permission from the government to perform with a foreign company. Since then, he has worked with ballet companies around the world. His performances have been widely televised and he now serves as both director and producer for several televised dance events.

Violette Verdy and Peter Schaufuss

Andris Liepa of the Bolshoi Ballet

Jennie Somogyi and Nikolaj Hübbe

Robert Schumann's Davidsbündlertänze

PREMIERE: JUNE 19, 1980
COMPANY: NEW YORK CITY BALLET
THEATER: NEW YORK STATE THEATER, NEW YORK

By Leigh Witchel

If there is such a thing as a "typical" Balanchine ballet, *Robert Schumann's Davidsbündlertänze* is not it. Even at the end of his career, Balanchine did not simply conduct business as usual. Rather than the beautiful dance structures he was known for that glittered like faceted gems, Balanchine created an intimate, emotional work for four couples to Schumann's piano pieces, the "Dances of the League of David." "David's League" was an imaginary society filled with Schumann's alter egos, particularly the extroverted and fiery Florestan and the gentle Eusebius, and the ballet is as changeable in mood as Schumann.

Balanchine acknowledged, even in the title, that the ballet drew from Schumann's troubled life, including his love of his wife and piano student Clara Wieck. It is set for four couples, further divided into two groupings that form the pillars of the work, one more prominent than the other. Peter Martins with Heather Watts and Ib Andersen with Kay Mazzo danced the two subsidiary couples, but the meat of the work is in the couplings of Karin von Aroldingen with Adam Lüders and Suzanne Farrell with Jacques d'Amboise.

Davidsbündlertänze takes place in a curtained pavilion, with the pianist onstage in period costume. Gnarled trees can be seen behind with water and a ghostly, luminous cathedral in the distance. Farrell and d'Amboise come running in. He asks a question, she evades a response. Lüders and von Aroldingen dance. She embraces him as if to kiss him, but lays her head on his shoulder instead. So much of *Davidsbündlertänze* is about embraces not completed, kisses not taken, words not spoken. It is, as dance critic Arlene Croce wrote after the premiere, as if we are not watching dances, but "a series of short, probing conversations." Even at their gayest, the dances have the pitch of hysteria in them. Gradually the women change into pointe shoes and the work churns toward its apex, a dance for Lüders in which Schumann is surrounded by Philistines, who appear in the form of black-cloaked critics with enormous books and quill pens. At the end, having changed back into heeled shoes, von Aroldingen leads Lüders on for the merest suspicion of a dance; they barely move at first beyond swaying. His pleasure in her company is obvious, but cannot last. His demons win as Robert backs off into darkness, leaving Clara alone to weep.

Mr. Balanchine and Sara Leland rehearse

Mr. Balanchine responds to a curtain call after premiere

Suzanne Farrell

Karin von Aroldingen and Adam Lüders

Even though stories can be teased out of the individual dances, Balanchine did not make a narrative ballet. He referred to Lüders's and von Aroldingen's roles specifically as "Robert" and "Clara," but then who are the other couples? It is never made plain; it was never meant to be. What Balanchine has given to us is not only a comment on Schumann's life, but on his times, the period of German Romanticism in which he lived. The atmosphere and mystery are part of the fascination of this most anguished and atypical of Balanchine's works. ᕉ

Leigh Witchel has written on Balanchine's choreography for Ballet Review, DanceView, *and* Dance Now. *A 2001 Guggenheim fellow in choreography and himself the creator of more than fifty ballets, Mr. Witchel is the founder of Dance as Ever, a ballet company based in Manhattan.*

New York City Ballet

Mr. Balanchine choreographing with Karin von Aroldingen and Adam Lüders

Mr. Balanchine choreographing with Karin von Aroldingen and Adam Lüders

Mr. Balanchine choreographing with Karin von Aroldingen and Adam Lüders

Mr. Balanchine choreographing with Karin von Aroldingen

Elyse Borne, Richard Dryden, Brian Pitts, Colleen Neary, Richard Tanner, Tracey Bennett

Rubies

Premiere: April 13, 1967
Company: New York City Ballet
Theater: City Center of Music and Drama, New York

By Robert Weiss

I wanted to dance *Rubies* since the first time I watched it being choreographed. I joined the New York City Ballet in the spring of 1966 and *Jewels* was one of the first new ballets that Mr. B worked on in 1967. Being a new member of the company I was of course in the corps of *Diamonds*, but I desperately wanted to be one of the four men in *Rubies*, which I got to dance my second season in the company.

I watched all the rehearsals that I could from under the piano in the main rehearsal hall. Unlike many choreographers, Balanchine was very generous in letting anyone who wanted to watch him work do so. I couldn't believe what I was seeing. Here was something really new—a totally classical ballet that really incorporated jazz in a seamless manner. It was so American—it had wit and sophistication and looked like so much fun to dance. It also had something else—Edward Villella, the dancer I most admired at that time in my life.

There were a lot of dancers to whom I looked up as I was growing up, including Rudolf Nureyev, Jacques d'Amboise, and Eric Bruhn, but if truth be told, the dancer I admired the most was Villella. Eddie was in the classical tradition but was also a "real" person on the stage. He communicated his emotions directly to the audience and drew you into the ballets he danced. He wasn't a typical prince or cavalier, although he could dance those roles as well. He was able to act through his body in a way I had never seen before. It was so thoroughly modern. In the numerous roles Mr. B created or revived for him, he left an indelible mark on all who came after him in those parts.

Damian Woetzel

Mr. Balanchine rehearses Patricia McBride and Robert Weiss

When *Jewels* premiered, *Rubies* was my favorite, although I loved them all. I went out front and stood with many of my colleagues in the back of the first ring of the theater and marveled with everyone else at Mr. B's inventiveness. (Being in the corps of *Diamonds* the men didn't have to dance until the last ten minutes of the evening so many of us watched *Emeralds* and *Rubies* from the front of the house.) It was always fascinating to see how Mr. B used the qualities of the dancers so extraordinarily well. Every part was choreographed for the uniqueness of each dancer.

I was the third male dancer in the company to dance the principal part in *Rubies*. After Villella, it was occasionally danced by John Clifford for a short time. When he left, I became the understudy to Eddie. But because of the company's busy schedule, there was never any time to rehearse. I hadn't even finished learning the part when Eddie's back went out right before the curtain went up on *Emeralds*. I probably had only two or three hours of rehearsal. By this time I was the first and only cast of the pas de trois in *Emeralds*. I was one of the four men in *Rubies* and I was still in the corps of *Diamonds*. The company was much smaller in 1967 and there were many more women than men.

I finished learning the role during the performance with Sara Leland (who was the second cast to Patricia McBride and scheduled to perform that afternoon with Villella). We went to the main hall during all of *Emeralds* when I was not needed on the stage. We continued right through the intermission with a brief time-out to change costumes. They even extended the intermission a bit. Sally talked me through the ballet as it was happening. She was always such a giving person and a real trouper. I was a nervous wreck but I still had a great time dancing the part. It was a challenge because I so admired Eddie. When he retired, the part was pretty much exclusively mine for several years and I found my own way of approaching it. I danced the role with a number of ballerinas including Heather Watts, who brought her own special gifts to the ballet, and McBride, who originated it.

Patricia McBride practices her steps with Mr. Balanchine

I was very excited when I was chosen by Mr. B to film the pas de deux with Patty for PBS's *Great Performances*.

Balanchine changed some of the choreography for television. He said the angles of the stage did not translate some of the movement well enough for TV. After seeing the changes, Balanchine decided he liked them better than the original. When we went back to the stage, Patty and I wanted to go back to the original choreography. Mr. B wanted to keep the changes made for TV. We couldn't understand why, as we felt so comfortable in the roles done in the old way; we really thought the original was better. Over the years I realized that Mr. B was right and we were just comfortable with what had been so familiar. Often dancers get stuck in a groove. Part of the genius of Balanchine as a choreographer was his ability to keep developing his work in new directions—not just his new work, but his revisions to the old as well. It was a great privilege to have worked with him and to have learned so much during some of his greatest creative years. ❧

Mr Balanchine demonstrates his choreography

Robert Weiss graduated from the School of American Ballet in 1966 at the age of sixteen and was asked to join the New York City Ballet that same year by George Balanchine. He danced as a principal in more than forty ballets in the company's repertory over a period of sixteen years. He went on to direct the Pennsylvania Ballet for almost a decade and since 1997, he has been the Founding Director of the Carolina Ballet in Raleigh, North Carolina. Mr.Weiss is also a teacher and choreographer with more than thirty ballets to his credit. He is married to ballerina Melissa Podcasy.

Mr. Balanchine rehearses Patricia McBride and Robert Weiss

Irina Golub of the Kirov Ballet

Maria Kowroski

Kyra Nichols and Lindsay Fischer

Scotch Symphony

PREMIERE: NOVEMBER 11, 1952
COMPANY: NEW YORK CITY BALLET
THEATER: CITY CENTER OF MUSIC AND DRAMA, NEW YORK

By Alexandra Tomalonis

Part *La Sylphide,* part *Brigadoon, Scotch Symphony* is one of Balanchine's sweetest and most enigmatic ballets. Created in 1952 for Maria Tallchief and André Eglevsky, it is one of several works Balanchine made to preserve something of ballet's history and to provide his company's repertory, which he often compared to a restaurant's menu, with an exotic dish representative of a particular style. The ballet is concocted from the steps, the conceits, and the atmosphere of the Romantic era with a sauce of heather and Highland mists.

The opening movement is danced in the village and dominated by a young woman, originally Patricia Wilde, who performs bravura beats with an almost masculine brilliance. The ballerina who appears in the second act is a sylphlike creature, alluring and mysterious, and the man dances under her spell. An atmosphere of melancholy and a sense of tragedy color this scene, although it is tragedy remembered, not as an active force.

Unlike James, the feckless hero of *La Sylphide,* who dares to dance with his dream and pays dearly, this cavalier can touch his sylph, and dances with her in a pas de deux. In an echo of feats that wowed nineteenth-century audiences, the ballerina seems to fly when the eight kilted men who guard her toss her to her partner. In the third movement, all vestiges of *La Sylphide* evaporate, as both the sylph and her swain lead the corps in a happy ending, a celebration of brilliant, joyous dancing.

If one takes it literally, the narrative thread of *Scotch Symphony* is too tenuous to be satisfying (who is the "little Scotch girl" and what happens to her

Kyra Nichols and Lindsay Fischer

Kirov Ballet rehearsal

after the first movement?). If one looks at the ballet as beautifully mellifluous choreography to Mendelssohn's symphony of the same name, it is greater than the sum of its disparate parts.

The central roles have been danced by a variety of artists. Tallchief was the New York City Ballet's prima ballerina in 1952, and had been regarded primarily as a brilliant technician. *Scotch Symphony* showed a different aspect of her artistry, revealing a softness of style and vulnerability of spirit. However, Balanchine did not seem particular about either the body type or personality of the dancer cast in the ballerina role, and subsequent interpreters included women as different as Diana Adams, Allegra Kent, Patricia McBride, and Suzanne Farrell. Similarly, Eglevsky's role was also danced by both Jacques d'Amboise and Edward Villella. After Wilde, the "little Scotch girl" was danced by Karin von Aroldingen and Sheryl Ware, among many others. She must be out there still, one supposes, dancing her flashing beats somewhere in Balanchine's infinite forest. ♪

Alexandra Tomalonis has reviewed dance for the Washington Post, Dance Magazine, *and other publications since 1979. She is editor of* DanceView *and* Ballet Alert!, *and the author of* Henning Kronstam, Portrait of a Danish Dancer *(University Press of Florida, 2002).*

Kirov Ballet rehearsal

Kyra Nichols and Lindsay Fischer with the New York City Ballet

Maya Dumchenko and Denis Firsov of the Kirov Ballet

Serenade

PREMIERE: MARCH 1, 1935
COMPANY: SCHOOL OF AMERICAN BALLET
THEATER: ADELPHI THEATER, NEW YORK

By Jean Battey Lewis

Was there ever such a corps de ballet as the one in *Serenade*? Think back on the grand, classic corps roles—the Shades scene of *La Bayadere* or the second act of *Swan Lake*. *Serenade* expands the splendor of those visions, the freedom of its movement and alert musical response sweeping us into a vibrant new world.

Consider the transfixing opening, with its diagonal rows of women in long, pale blue tutus, their right arms raised to shield their eyes from the light of the moon; the piercing moment when, standing with feet together, they suddenly shift into first position and you see the transformation of young women into ballet dancers. It is a movement so simple yet so suggestive that when Martha Graham first saw it, she is reported to have said that tears came to her eyes because it was a simplicity that was the mark of a master.

The choreographic patterns Balanchine unfolds are thrilling: women moving at top speed in dizzying pirouettes coalescing into a circle; the entrance of four dancers, and the piling up of visual images as the four are joined by three others, one by one, making a blossoming bouquet; the great climactic moment early on when the dancers, on a long diagonal, swirl offstage like a huge rolling wave in a froth of arms and flyaway skirts.

It is amusing to hear Balanchine, the master craftsman, describe some of the technical hurdles of composition in this, the first ballet he created in this country, as he dealt with a fledgling group of dancers who often showed up for rehearsals in haphazard fashion. One night seventeen women were there: "The problem was how to arrange this odd number of girls so that they would look interesting. I placed them on diagonal lines and decided that the hands should move

Uliana Lopatkina, Sofia Gumerova, and Denis Firsov of the Kirov Ballet

Kirk Petersen of the National Ballet of Washington

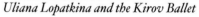

Uliana Lopatkina and the Kirov Ballet

Uliana Lopatkina and Denis Firsov of the Kirov Ballet

Sofia Gumerova of the Kirov Ballet

first to give the girls practice. One day, when all the girls rushed off the floor area we were using as a stage, one of the girls fell and began to cry. I kept this bit in the dance. Another day, one of the girls was late for class, so I left that in too." It is a good example of art defying analysis.

Balanchine's description pales beside the mystery and passion we see onstage: a man entering, "blinded" by a fate figure; later the great beating of arms, like large wings, by a woman who is guiding his destiny; a ballerina on pointe in arabesque, slowly revolving as her leg is turned by a partner half hidden behind her long skirt; the final picture of a dancer lifted high in the air by three men, who carry her like an infant as she spreads her arms backward, handmaidens following her slowly on pointe as she is borne heavenward.

Later in his life, having trained audiences to see movement for itself, not as incidental to a dramatic plot, Balanchine would allow that there was more

New York City Ballet

to *Serenade* than happy accident. He wrote, "The apparently 'pure' dance takes on a kind of plot. But this plot, inherent in the score, contains many stories—it is many things to many listeners to the music, and many things to many people who see the ballet." Then he added, "Making a ballet is a choreographer's way of showing how he understands a piece of music."

For its hauntingly lovely response to Tchaikovsky's score, for its energy and ardor, for its subtle but haunting evocation of figures caught in the hand of fate, for its exaltation of women to what Balanchine felt was their ideal state of grace as ballet heroines, *Serenade* exerts a timeless spell. It retains the freshness of youth seventy years after it was first created. ❧

Jean Battey Lewis is a dance critic based in Washington.

Maya Dumchenko of the Kirov Ballet

New York City Ballet

Uliana Lopatkina, Veronika Part, Maya Dumchenko, and
Denis Firsov of the Kirov Ballet

New York City Ballet

Maria Kowroski

Kirov Ballet

Maria Kowroski and Damian Woetzel

Slaughter on Tenth Avenue

PREMIERE: MAY 2, 1968
COMPANY: NEW YORK CITY BALLET
THEATER: NEW YORK STATE THEATER, NEW YORK

By Doris Hering

"Americana"—an artistic pursuit at once tough and sentimental. It has turned up in works including Humphrey's *Song of the West*, Charles Weidman's *A House Divided*, and Paul Taylor's *Company B*.

These are all American choreographers; there is logic in their affection. But George Balanchine, who was not born in this country, has an even more abiding affection for American mores, and in some of his works with American subject matter, he came closer to the core than his native-born colleagues. Among these are *Western Symphony*, with its tongue-in-cheek glance at cowboys and their beruffled ladies; *Stars and Stripes*, with its Fourth of July zest; and *Ivesiana*, with its darker view.

These were created for the ballet stage. His first piece for the musical comedy stage was a touching and, at the same time, amusing opus called *Slaughter on Tenth Avenue*. It was a self-contained dance episode in the show called *On Your Toes* (Act II, scene 4). Here Balanchine, not long in this country, caught the flavor of a sleazy saloon in Hell's Kitchen on the West Side of Manhattan. Little did he know that this very neighborhood would eventually house the New York City Ballet, not that *Slaughter on Tenth Avenue* pretended to be a social study.

Unlike the Broadway shows that preceded it, *On Your Toes* did not use dancers as window dressing; they were an integral part of both the dramatic and danced fabric. Furthermore, Balanchine, who at that time spoke limited English, knew enough to persuade the producer, Dwight Deere Wiman, to change the credit from the usual "Dances by" to "Choreography by."

The original version of this rat-a-tat tale was premiered at the Imperial Theater on April 11, 1936. The spirited Tamara Geva, who had been Balanchine's first wife, portrayed Vera Barnova, a striptease girl. Ray Bolger, as Phil Dolan III, was her tap-dancing admirer. The dance was created around the backstage life of a ballet company and the newfound love of Vera and Phil. Three years later, Balanchine was invited to restage *On Your Toes* for Warner Brothers in Hollywood. This time, Vera Zorina and Eddie Albert, Jr. were the principals. The tap dancing was dubbed.

Suzanne Farrell and Christopher d'Amboise

Suzanne Farrell and Christopher d'Amboise

Thirty years later, *Slaughter on Tenth Avenue* reappeared as an independent work in the New York City Ballet repertory. Although Balanchine retained the story by Richard Rodgers, Lorenz Hart, and George Abbott, and the Rodgers score of which he was very fond, he completely revised the choreography to suit the more finely honed talents of Suzanne Farrell and Arthur Mitchell, who was as sharp a tapper as he was a classical dancer.

Broadway reclaimed *On Your Toes* in 1983 with choreography by Balanchine aided by Peter Martins. Natalia Makarova and Lara Teeter were Vera and Phil, and Makarova received a Tony Award for her performance.

Slaughter is still in the New York City Ballet repertory. It is currently danced by Maria Kowroski with Damian Woetzel and Philip Neal. In 2002 it was also a vehicle briefly for guest artist Sofiane Sylve.

Maria Kowroski and Damian Woetzel

Maria Kowroski

Despite these numerous manifestations—and there have been others—*Slaughter* is not a major Balanchine ballet. Nevertheless, it is remarkable in its marshalling of nuggets of Americana, like the slouching gangsters, the stripper with the heart of a lady, the stomping cops, and the humorous concept of the hoofer who avoids being shot by tapping without missing a beat—added proof of how Balanchine believed in the power of dance.

In 1945 Doris Hering joined Dance Magazine *as associate editor and principal critic. From 1972–1987, she served as founding executive director of the National Assoication for Regional Ballet and then returned to the magazine as a senior editor. She is the recepient of several awards, among them the Capezio Award, Martha Hill Award, Dance Critics Assoication Award, two Howard D. Rothschild Fellowships, and the Sage Cowles Land Grant Chair in Dance. Her most recent book is* Giselle and Albrecht: American Ballet Theatre's Romantic Lovers.

Maria Kowroski

Maria Kowroski and Damian Woetzel

Wendy Whelan and Nikolaj Hübbe

La Sonnambula

PREMIERE: JANUARY 26, 1960
COMPANY: NEW YORK CITY BALLET
THEATER: CITY CENTER OF MUSIC AND DRAMA, NEW YORK

By Paul Parish

There are several "families" of Balanchine ballets. The great neo-classical line leads from *The Four Temperaments* through *Agon* and *Episodes* to *Stravinsky Violin Concerto*. Another, its Romantic complement, leads from *Night Shadow* (*La Sonnambula*) through *The Unanswered Question, Meditation,* and *Don Quixote* to *Robert Schumann's Davidsbündlertänze.* In these poignant ballets we see the Ideal Woman—eternally beautiful—but we also get a glimpse of the artist himself, tragically doomed never to grasp the object of his adoration. This line is perhaps the most important of all; Balanchine himself danced the role of Don Quixote. As he told Francis Mason, "Everything a man does he does for his ideal woman; you live only one life and you believe in something and I believe in that."

The ancestor of Don Quixote, and of this whole family of ballets, is the poet in *Night Shadow;* his beloved is oblivious to him. The poet "smiles, but she doesn't see, she just doesn't see." Danilova danced the sleepwalking heroine in the original Ballet Russe production of *Night Shadow* in 1946. The story was shaped by its composer, Vittorio Rieti, who based it on Bellini's opera La Sonnambula, whence the name by which the ballet now usually called. The story is stark: A poet is invited to the palace of a magnifico; the nobleman's mistress toys with him, the guests look him over but laugh at him, the mysterious lady of the house crosses his path and fascinates him—but the nobleman (tipped off by the mistress) revenges himself on the intruding poet and kills him. The poet has entered a great world in which he can never belong. He is, as Balanchine said of himself (quoting the revolutionary poet Mayakovsky, his contemporary), "a cloud in trousers" —one for whom the ideal can not be realized in this life. The nebulous and the tangible cannot meet—and yet we *can* see the conflict.

She drifts across the stage on pointe, barely touching the ground, like a feather on a breeze. She bourrées with tiny nibbling steps, holding a tall candle absolutely upright, like the image of an obsession, and floats, right up against the poet's body, who in his fascination with her has thrown himself prone onto the floor. He lies there like a log in her path, she stops, and with immense delicacy steps over him and continues on her mysterious way. He cannot get through to her.

Perhaps the greatest dancers in the roles, Allegra Kent as the sleepwalker and Henning Kronstam as the poet who loves her, never performed in the same productions, but they are each others' counterparts with such integrity, such

fidelity to the world of the imagination, the artist's calling. "You're lost before you enter," said Kronstam about his art. "You're very alone, this excitement and . . . this breathlessness . . . . [The art is to] suddenly transform all this knowledge into an experience. What we long for is the unexpected."

Kent had fantastic success with the role with New York City Ballet (especially when they toured Russia). Kronstam danced his role for twenty years, his whole

Mr. Balanchine backstage before performance

Wendy Whelan

career, in the Royal Danish Ballet in Copenhagen. Each was out of this world in the ballet, fantastically alive onstage. Kent has been taped coaching Darci Kistler in the role, teaching the young dancer how to be blind to the poet's presence yet somehow aware: "It's like echolocation; you can't see him, but you know he's there."

The poet Edwin Denby, who wrote about the ballet when it was new, compared it to a story by Edgar Allan Poe. "It gives you a sense of losing your bearings, the feeling of an elastic sort of time and a heaving floor. As a friend of mine remarked, 'when it's over, you don't know what's hit you.'" ⁓

Paul Parish grew up in Mississippi, where he was the best rock-and-roll dancer in his high school. He began writing about the Royal Ballet in letters home while studying in England as a Rhodes Scholar, and has since written for Ballet Review, Ballett International/Tanz Aktuell *(Berlin),* San Francisco, *and alternative papers in the Bay Area. He studies ballet with Sally Streets and Susan Weber.*

Mr. Balanchine rehearses John Taras, Jean-Pierre Frohlich, Victor Castelli, Karin von Aroldingen, and Shaun O'Brien

Wendy Whelan and Nikolaj Hübbe

John Taras looks on as Mr. Balanchine rehearses before a show

Jennifer Ringer and Peter Boal

La Source

PREMIERE: NOVEMBER 23, 1968
COMPANY: NEW YORK CITY BALLET
THEATER: NEW YORK STATE THEATER, NEW YORK

by Violette Verdy

One day Balanchine surprised me by saying, "I need your help." He wanted to do a new piece for me and John Prinz, a very brilliant but wild, beautiful-looking young dancer. And Mr. B said, "The boy is very talented, but he doesn't know how to present himself yet, and I want to work with him and reveal him and give him the details of presentation: partnering, walking, how to run offstage, how to enter." He told me I would have to be there a lot, to be patient while John learned partnering, but I would have the pleasure of seeing him develop. Balanchine said, "I need you to be a French hostess."

So Mr. B started and I immediately realized how beautiful the music was. Delibes is such a great composer, and he embodies so much of what France considered high qualities—both nobility and the tenderness of feeling between men and women. It was all in the music. Our first pas de deux was to a beautiful little cello concerto; the voice of the cello is grave and serious, yet tender.

When we first danced *La Source,* the form was two pas de deux and two variations each. Each of the pas de deux has a little introduction, a tradition of nineteenth-century ballet and opera—introducing the public to the next piece by preparing them. You hear birds calling and you know somebody's about to enter the scene. Or there is a cloud in front of the sun; three drops of water fall down, but it is all going to clear when they come in. That is how it was. There was a little introduction and then you began to dance or you made your entrance. It was like a fastidious nineteenth-century letter: the formality of beginning a letter, closing it, addressing it properly, when you have a comma, when you have a period.

The first solo I had was delicious because it was so aerial, very light and sharp, and very beautiful. John's solo allowed him to introduce a more leisurely, elegant aspect of himself, not just the force, not just the power and the raw energy.

And then we had another pas de deux that was much more contemporary, less intimate, more of a showpiece. And two more solos. John had a more buoyant solo, a mazurka, and again, it was melodious. My solo did not use a huge variety of steps but there were some delicious little things in it. One was jumping on pointe and then unexpectedly not on pointe, but by the time you deciphered it, the little charade was over. And another was dancing over a phrase of music using different counts than the musical beats and finishing on time—a little syncopated thing. It made use of nineteenth-century ballet language—entrechat quatre, passés on pointe, relevés on pointe—all done with elegant arms and presentation.

Originally there was no introduction, no finale, and no corps. After the first performances, Balanchine added some other dances he had already choreographed to Delibes's music. He salvaged them to give us some rest between our pas de deux and solos, and he introduced a regular finale, a wonderful waltz that served for the corps to dance, and for us to make entrances in and to participate in the ending with the corps. Mr. B's idea of France in *La Source* was almost a platonic ideal of the French. It was France through the eyes of an educated person from St. Petersburg who remembered how much France and Russia had in common and how much France brought to Russia with Catherine and the tsar and all the artists that came to St. Petersburg—Petipa, Didelot, the builders, and the constructors. The city is built like a beautiful theater, like Paris is a theater. Balanchine thought of the Paris Opera Ballet only as the temple of dance, although for the French it was also the bordello of France—a most expensive, beautiful, and refined bordello for the men who came looking for mistresses.

For me dancing *La Source* was being home once more. The movements Mr. B gave me and that music—they are like family, they are in my genes.

Violette Verdy danced more than 25 principal roles in a performance career that lasted from 1958 through 1976. In 1977, Miss Verdy became the first woman appointed Artistic Dancer of the Paris Opera Ballet; she served in that capacity until 1980 when she became Co-Artistic Director of the Boston Ballet. In 1984, she returned to New York City Ballet, where she held the title of Teaching Associate. In addition to teaching at NYCB, Miss Verdy accepted teaching residencies and choreographic commissions at various institutions of higher education and at national and international dance companies. Since August of 1996, Miss Verdy has been a full-time Professor of Ballet at the School of Music at Indiana University, Bloomington, and contributes as Artistic Advisor for the Rock School of Ballet in Philadelphia, Pennsylvania.

Abi Stafford

Jennie Somogyi

Kyra Nichols

Square Dance

Premiere: November 21, 1957
Company: New York City Ballet
Theater: New York State Theater, New York

by Patricia Wilde

Mr. B had just returned to the company after a year with Tanny [Tanaquil Le Clercq] in Copenhagen. He started work on *Square Dance, Agon,* and I believe, *Gounod Symphony.* On any one day he might work on all three totally different ballets—quite amazing.

While working with me, Mr. B never said "This ballet is for you," but day by day the excitement grew

with the role, using a caller and the orchestra, in Western shirts, onstage. He was creating (not his word, he always said "only God creates, I make") something quite different for the new season.

My husband Youra and I spent weekends in Weston with Mr. B. They had many projects— carpentry, building and, of course, cooking. Often on

Sunday, the caller, Elisha Keeler, and his wife came to dinner, I would mark various sequences of *Square Dance,* and Keeler would work out calls for the steps. He would then come to rehearsals and try them with the music and choreography.

Mr. B rarely said how he wanted steps done, just "dance and really move!" However, in the second

New York City Ballet

Bart Cook

movement's slow beginning, he insisted on very deep pliés and long stretched movement which, for me, was the most difficult part. In performance with the orchestra platform stage right, we no longer had our usual center stage. This, combined with Keeler's calls, which at times did not match my steps, was problematic. Later, dancer Robert Lindgren did the calls very well. Finally, I performed the present version, with no caller and no musicians onstage, only the beautiful male solo was not as yet added.

Later, when I presented *Square Dance* at Pittsburgh Ballet Theatre, we included the male solo, which gave the ballerina a lovely breather after the girls' dance and into the coda.

One other change: during my performances, the second entrance of the principal girl was a jeté elonge demi-tour and immediately a second jeté elonge demi-tour—continuously in a clockwise circle to upstage center. This is a difficult sequence but has a terrific bounce and very unique drive. *Square Dance* was a joyous experience. Mr. B wanted it to be fun.

Patricia Wilde began her career at the age of fourteen with the Marquis de Cuevas Ballet International. She spent 15 years as a principal dancer with the New York City Ballet and worked closely with George Balanchine. Making eight international tours with the company, she has danced at the Bolshoi, La Scala, Covent Garden, and the Paris Opera. She served twelve years as a coach and teacher for the American Ballet Theatre School and was appointed Director in 1979. Ms. Wilde joined the Pittsburgh Ballet Theatre as Artistic Director in 1982, and although she retired in 1997, she still serves as an Artist Advisor.

Sebastien Marcovici

Kyra Nichols

Manuel Legris of the Paris Opera Ballet

left and right: Ethan Stiefel shines in Stars and Stripes

Stars and Stripes

PREMIERE: JANUARY 17, 1958
COMPANY: NEW YORK CITY BALLET
THEATER: CITY CENTER OF MUSIC AND DRAMA, NEW YORK

by Gia Kourlas

George Balanchine understood that vulgarity, by definition, could also mean something wonderful. Watching his 1958 *Stars and Stripes* is a bit like seeing New York City Ballet in drag. In an impressive, insanely bold theatrical style, it both defies and embraces the notion of vulgarity. The ballet, paired with the rousing marches of John Philip Sousa (as adapted and orchestrated by Hershy Kay), could never be considered understated, but that is why it is so glorious. In its five movements (wittily dubbed "campaigns"), *Stars and Stripes* embodies all that is good about America. There is eternal optimism, the spirit and freedom of jazz, an affectionate nod to the Rockettes, and purposely terrible bad taste. It could work as part of the half-time show at the Super Bowl. The title is adorable, but it could just as easily have been called *Fireworks* and not simply because of Karinska's glittering costumes. This ballet boils over with difficult variations, fast footwork, and a grand pas de deux to die for. And it was also unbelievably subtle. Underneath all the glitter, *Stars and Stripes* is a real ballet.

Nearly forty-five years after its creation, the glitter has not faded from Balanchine's patriotic confection. At the same time it is clear that it could not be created today. Balanchine was an immigrant and from the Western ties he wore to his admiration for American icon Fred Astaire, it is obvious that he adored his adopted country. But

New York City Ballet

Damian Woetzel

as with every Balanchine ballet, the music counts for everything. He makes Sousa's marches seem less like background material for a car commercial than a serious ballet score. In a fuzzy black-and-white clip from the *Dance in America* presentation of The Balanchine Celebration, the choreographer discusses his fixation: "Sousa is a composer that was a pupil of Offenbach—he played viola in Offenbach's orchestra," he said. "He wrote French Offenbachian type of music. The marches that he wrote were adopted here by our army. It's 120 metronome, which is a French march—it's very fast walking. Do you see

New York City Ballet

French people walk? They walk like mad! See, that's how Americans walk. Why? Because of Sousa!"

That sort of tenderness is at the root of *Stars and Stripes.* In the final moments, when the flag rises, filling the entire back of the stage, it is hard not to buy into Balanchine's vision, hook, line, and sinker. It is cornball heaven, MGM musical style—earnest and flashy—but never tacky or sentimental. *Stars and Stripes* is a celebration created by a choreographer who was not only a genius but also an unabashed patriot. ❦

Gia Kourlas is the Dance Editor of Time Out New York.

Merrill Ashley

New York City Ballet

Patricia McBride and Mikhail Baryshnikov

The Steadfast Tin Soldier

PREMIERE: JULY 30, 1975
COMPANY: NEW YORK CITY BALLET
THEATER: SARATOGA PERFORMING ARTS CENTER, SARATOGA SPRINGS, NEW YORK

By Robert Johnson

Although sometimes dismissed as a trifle, *The Steadfast Tin Soldier* continues to move audiences with its quirky tale of love that goes awry. The ballet's protagonists are humble—just a toy soldier and the paper-doll ballerina whom he adores. Yet their commonness increases the ballet's sentimental appeal.

George Balanchine choreographed the duet in a hurry, loosely basing his work on a story of the same name by Hans Christian Andersen. For music, Balanchine chose selections from Georges Bizet's *Jeux d'Enfants*, employing a brisk march to suggest the soldier's profession and associating his love interest with a drowsy lullaby.

David Mitchell designed the scenery and costumes. The set depicts an antique parlor with a Christmas tree and toys arranged on either side of a crackling hearth. This cozy, December scene made its debut peculiarly in high summer: the Saratoga Performing Arts Center, in Saratoga Springs, New York, commissioned the piece for New York City Ballet's summer season there.

To our left, the ballerina appears poised with her face tilted, as though expecting a kiss. On the other side, the soldier stands stiffly at the head of a painted regiment. He steps forward, and turns, rocking on his heels, evincing from the outset the unsteadiness of love. Later, he nearly topples over, falling to his knee to kiss her hand. Gentle humor stems from such mishaps. The dolls' awkward mannerisms at once undercut and enhance the virtuosity of the classical steps Balanchine gives them to perform in their respective solos and in a trickily balanced adagio.

Despite their stylization, both characters are subtly emotional. While the soldier appears earnest, the ballerina has a mischievous personality. When she finishes her pirouettes softly, she claps her hands in delight, peering to the side to see if anyone has noticed. He nearly collapses when he makes his declaration of love, but she raises him up, and soothes him. Together they express their innermost dreams. She rocks an imaginary baby, and he swells with pride,

smoothing his mustache. After he presents his heart to her—a candy-red token—the lovers celebrate with a ballet promenade whose solemnity is only slightly skewed by her flexed foot.

The adagio gives way to high-spirited sequences of turns, like a formal coda. As the dancers' energies mount, it grows hot in the room. Heedless of danger, the ballerina throws open the window, and the

Patricia McBride and Mikhail Baryshnikov

curtains billow violently. All night long, the dolls have teetered off-balance, reaching for a happiness that seems beyond their limits. Finally they lose control. The wind whisks the ballerina, who is merely a paper cutout, into the burning fireplace, where she disappears entirely.

The soldier's tin heart remains unconsumed, however, lying in the embers. With an air of disbelief, he reaches to extract it, and he wipes away a tear as he slips the heart back inside his uniform. The tin soldier resumes his place at the head of his regiment. Upright and heroic, he guards his secret sorrows. Even a toy, it seems, can have a past. At this point the ballet reproduces in miniature the theme of elusive love, and heartbreak that appears in Balanchine's most intense, neo-Romantic works, such as the "Elegie" section of *Tchaikovsky Suite No. 3.*

At the premiere of *The Steadfast Tin Soldier,* Danish dancer Peter Schaufuss played the tin soldier. A mercurial presence, and new to the company, he had to confine his personality within this role.

Although susceptible to love, the soldier must maintain his stoicism. Understatement is the essence of his character.

Patricia McBride created the role of the ballerina doll. This debut followed her triumph as Swanilda in *Coppélia,* performed at Saratoga Springs the previous summer. The ten-minute duet seemed like a pendant to the evening-length ballet in which she also impersonated a doll. McBride has commented that her challenge was to create a different kind of doll in *The Steadfast Tin Soldier.* She was shy, but hopeful, and giddily impetuous. Some balletomanes had labeled

McBride a "soubrette." Other observers, however, noted that she possessed a darker, womanly side. Among the finest Balanchine ballerinas, McBride could shade her stage persona with depths of mystery.

Both McBride and Schaufuss brought an extra dimension to the characters in *The Steadfast Tin Soldier,* which may have been the point of casting such sophisticated artists in those roles, for the characters are not as simple as they seem. Often, the doll's mask hints at what lies behind or beyond. Stylization points to universal humanity.

Patricia McBride and Mikhail Baryshnikov

In creating a "doll" ballet, Balanchine had recourse to the symbolist traditions of the Ballets Russes whence he came. Precedents include not only the original staging of *Jeux d'Enfants* by Léonide Massine (Balanchine rechoreographed this ballet in 1955), but also Michel Fokine's *Petrouchka,* and even Fokine's *Le Carnaval,* where at one point Harlequin offers his heart to Columbine. In the same genre were earlier stagings of the ballet *The Fairy Doll,* at the Maryinsky Theater in St. Petersburg.

In *The Steadfast Tin Soldier,* viewers may identify with the dreams of creatures strangely flawed, but who still yearn for love, and desire to become fully human. At the same time, and with equal poignancy, the ballet shows us human beings in the innocent guise of dolls. By these means, *The Steadfast Tin Soldier* offers the mature yet wistful perception that all of us are really children when we fall in love. ✎

Robert Johnson is the dance critic of The Star-Ledger *(Newark, New Jersey) and has written and lectured about dance for many years.*

Mr. Balanchine rehearses Mikhail Baryshnikov

Patricia McBride and Mikhail Baryshnikov

Karin von Aroldingen and Bart Cook

Stravinsky Violin Concerto

PREMIERE: JUNE 18, 1972
COMPANY: NEW YORK CITY BALLET
THEATER: STRAVINSKY FESTIVAL, NEW YORK STATE THEATER, NEW YORK

By Susan Jaffe

From 1980 to 1989, one of the greatest legends of the dance world, Mikhail Baryshnikov, took the artistic directorship of The American Ballet Theatre. One of the things he wanted to accomplish was to bring in more varied ballets to create more well rounded dancers as well as audiences. Mischa was a big fan of George Balanchine, and he brought quite a few Balanchine works to ABT. This was wonderful for us because dancing his ballets was quite an enriching experience. There was really no other choreographer that I could say matched Balanchine's incredible musicality with such intricate perfection. Sometimes I would stop with complete wonderment at how Mr. B could come up with a particular step for that particular passage of music. It was as if there was no other step on earth that could be better for that passage of music. He had tapped into the universal mind and saw what step needed to be in that place at that time as if it were already waiting for him.

Stravinsky Violin Concerto was one of those sublime ballets. Mind you, it was murder to count! I will never forget this one place in the finale where if we didn't count we wouldn't know when to start dancing no matter how many times we had danced the ballet. And to make matters worse, while we were counting we were facing the audience in a fixed pose so one had to make sure that one wasn't counting with one's mouth. I used to laugh to myself thinking that the audience could see the glazed look over my face frozen with the concentration of counting. Oh, how that moment made me nervous!

I danced the first pas de deux, which was the one he created for Kay Mazzo. It was the more lyrical of the two pas de deux he created for the central part

Wendy Whelan and Jock Soto

Mr. Balanchine rehearses

of the ballet. It is breathtakingly beautiful and the theme of it is a man supporting the ballerina as if to protect and keep her out of danger. There is a wonderful moment when the ballerina starts to drop to her knees but the man suddenly slides underneath her to catch her before she falls. There is a very tender and romantic quality to the first pas de deux. At the close of this movement, the man takes the woman's forehead with his hand as he is standing behind her and gently guides her into a backbend as he kneels down. There is just the most beautiful quality of surrender, that is mirrored by the music. The Stravinsky score is the violin, which is the predominant sound, and is as much full of pathos and beauty as it is sharp. Wonderfully angular, the shrill of the violin screams and then evolves into the most glorious heartache of a melody while still remaining simple and stark.

Mr. Balanchine rehearses

The other pas de deux was more bizarre and athletic with the movements of a gymnast. There were even bridges where the dancer is on her hands and feet in a backbend traveling across the floor. Leslie Browne and Ricardo Bustamente were opposite me in my cast and they were extraordinary to watch. The two of them just seemed to understand the essence of this dynamic and strange pas de deux, and I loved watching them from the wings. Then the finale came into full fervor with many dancers bending and weaving in and out as they were counting like mad from the wings before their entrances. Very intricate and complex, it was like dancing in an Escher painting! What an extraordinary ballet! 🖎

Susan Jaffe retired in June 2002 after a 22-year career as Principal Ballerina with the American Ballet Theatre. Plucked from the corps de ballet at a very early age, she was catapulted to stardom by her long-time mentor Mikhail Baryshnikov, who was director of ABT from 1980 to 1989. She has since made many classical ballets her signature and has danced as a guest artist with many European companies. She has also worked with and danced ballets by luminary choreographers such as Twyla Tharp, Yuri Kylian, Kenneth MacMillian, Nacho Duato, Anthony Tudor, Roland Petit, George Balanchine, John Cranko, Lar Lubovitch, and Agnes De Mille. She now acts as Advisor to the Chairman and President of the Board of Governing Trustees of American Ballet Theatre.

Mr. Balanchine rehearses Kay Mazzo and Peter Martins

Mr. Balanchine rehearses Kay Mazzo and Peter Martins

Mr. Balanchine rehearses Kay Mazzo and Peter Martins

New York City Ballet

Karin von Aroldingen and Bart Cook

Isabelle Guerin of the Paris Opera Ballet

Darcey Bussell of the Royal Ballet (U.K.)

Swan Lake

Premiere: November 20, 1951
Company: New York City Ballet
Theater: City Center of Music and Drama, New York

by Robert Greskovic

George Balanchine reputedly once suggested that all ballets should be called "Swan Lake" because the title had unbeatable popularity and "people would come." Still, Balanchine himself resisted the temptation to put on a version of Tchaikovsky's internationally famous 1877 score until 1951. The appearance of this "classic" on the stage of Balanchine's New York City Ballet, established in 1948 but underway since Balanchine emigrated to the United States in the late 1930s, came as something of a surprise, or a shock, depending on who was reacting. In the process of pursuing his vision of ballet in the United States, building on his beginnings in Russia and his subsequent development as choreographer in Western Europe, Balanchine had stressed a visionary sense of the new and the largely unpredictable, as far as ballet fare was concerned.

The initial appearance and subsequent life of Balanchine's *Swan Lake,* one act long and not called "Swan Lake, Act II," as is still carelessly done after the then-popular and ubiquitous staging seen near and far in the United States and Europe, proved to be atypically controversial. From just about any other ballet company, *Swan Lake* seemed a perfectly predictable presentation. Not so in the case of Balanchine's New York City Ballet. As enthusiasts of Balanchine's new-look ballets puzzled over what the master of contemporary ballet was doing with this old-world warhorse, traditionalists, suspicious of Balanchine's sense of exploration and invention regarding academic dancing, largely looked askance at the temerity of choreographic tampering with a sacrosanct artifact of ballet history.

Darcey Bussell of the Royal Ballet (U.K.)

Darci Kistler

Darcey Bussell of the Royal Ballet (U.K.) and Igor Zelensky of the Kirov Ballet

Balanchine revised his 1951 *Swan Lake,* with its accents on the narrative's swan maidens and on their lakeside appearances, several times between 1956 and 1980. Because his choreography for the ensemble of swan maidens treated their presence with renewed force and dramatic energy, some saw the corps de ballet as becoming a dominant force, even overshadowing Odette, the narrative's Swan Queen and the ballet's centerpiece. In fact, the sometimes wild force of Balanchine's artistically active swan corps only served to put Odette in higher relief. Overall, she sometimes stood out even more brilliantly for her emphatic body language, or, conversely, the ballerina, originally the indelible Maria Tallchief, electrified the full-stage picture by her riveting calm, giving off a gravely tragic aura and establishing herself with glacial coolness as the eye of a hurricane.

Striking and prime examples of such contrasts reveal themselves in Balanchine's choreographic reshaping of the ballet's great "love duet" for Odette and her prince, Siegfried: At a climactic moment, the Swan Queen extends an achingly taut, sky-reaching arabesque out of a slow and unusually configured promenade, all of which then concludes with a lavish burst of seemingly

Darcey Bussell of the Royal Ballet (U.K.) and Igor Zelensky of the Kirov Ballet

uncontainable energy marvelously timed to the explosive coda Tchaikovsky originally wrote, and that Balanchine reinstated in place of the then-familiar traditional and softened ending, specifically composed by Riccardo Drigo after Tchaikovsky's death.

Shading all the brilliant theatrics of Balanchine's encapsulation of the historic *Swan Lake* are equally effective low-key moments, such as the presence of hunters along the edges of the stage during the "Love Duet," wherein they provide loving shoulders on which the swan maidens can longingly rest their heads. And probably most moving of all is the ballet's tender, tragic ending, when, to the shimmering apotheosis Tchaikovsky wrote to conclude the complete ballet's last act, Odette caressingly blesses and lowers her prince's head to keep him from fixing on her inevitable departure, all of which transpires as a grandly delicate exit—no borrowings from the clichéd "Dying Swan" here. Odette reverses the path of her first entrance and climactically turns upstage, where, embellished by a sweeping flourish of her wing-like arms, she departs in profile, head raised, fully facing her fate.

Darcey Bussell of the Royal Ballet (U.K.) and Igor Zelensky of the Kirov Ballet

Darci Kistler and Igor Zelensky of the Kirov Ballet

Robert Greskovic is the author of Ballet 101, *and writes about dance for* The Wall Street Journal.

Maria Kowroski and Igor Zelensky with members of the New York City Ballet

Symphony in C

PREMIERE: MARCH 22, 1948
COMPANY: BALLET SOCIETY
THEATER: CITY CENTER OF MUSIC AND DRAMA, NEW YORK

By Nina Ananiashvili

Before I came to perform in America with the New York City Ballet in 1988, I had no idea of what to expect. When I was very young, Balanchine's works were not performed in Georgia [USSR]. I remember, as though it were a dream, going with my father to see a performance because Balanchine and his ballet had come to Georgia. But I did not pay much attention because I was not aware of Balanchine at that time. Before coming to America, I saw only *Apollo* on tape because it was more popular in Europe. When I came here, I first saw *Symphony in C* and *Raymonda Variations* on video and I thought, "Oh my God, are we crazy to come do all this difficult stuff for ten days? I want to go back!" I was so nervous and so confused. But we did not have any other choice. So we [Nina and fellow Soviet dancer Andris Liepa] came here.

It was so difficult to come here and do this. I ended up not just dancing, but learning, because the ballet was so quick—there were so many steps and they were absolutely new steps for me. At the Bolshoi, we do not have this quick technique and footwork like in *Symphony in C* and all of Balanchine's ballets. So it was really something. And if you have never danced Balanchine before in your life and then to come and just learn everything for a week and perform, I think it is really hard to do this ballet. This was really, really hard for me. I did not believe we could learn everything in such a short time. But because we did not have any other choice, we started working, and we worked like hell. And everybody in the company helped us.

I had two teachers, Sally [Leland] and Suzie [Hendl]. Sally taught *Raymonda* and Suzie taught

Symphony. And Peter Martins, of course. When we finally performed the ballets, I was the happiest person in the world because I knew we were doing something grandiose. I felt as though all of New York, all of America, was watching us. As though we were guinea pigs in an experimental lab and everyone wanted to see how it would come out.

Raymonda Variations was very difficult because it was the first piece performed. Because I danced *Raymonda* before, I knew the music and steps so well. But the steps were different for the New York City Ballet performance, which made it extra difficult. I always wanted to move my way, not the new way. Part of the difficulty was because we worked so hard on *Symphony in C*, it did not leave as much time to do

Raymonda. I told my instructors to really work with me so I could dance like it should be—like Patricia Wilde had done in the original at City Ballet. We worked so well and when I am dancing, I enjoy it very much. I had a wonderful partner, Otto Neubert. He really took care of me, even if it meant pulling me down to the floor. We worked together so beautifully and so wonderfully.

Now, I feel much better and more comfortable with *Symphony in C*. This is one of my favorite ballets to dance onstage. I like the music so much. I feel like Balanchine played this music onstage with the dancers. The notes from Bizet jump off the stage in the form of girls and boys. When I listen to this music, I cannot imagine other movements or other

The Bolshoi Ballet

The Bolshoi Ballet

ballets. I cannot even think about it. Immediately, Balanchine's *Symphony in C* comes to mind. I think this is one of his greatest ballets.

After the 1988 performance, it was my dream to have *Symphony in C* at the Bolshoi. At that time I thought our company could dance it very beautifully because we had beautiful boys, beautiful girls, very nice-looking people. It was my dream to bring

Veronika Part and Ilya Kuznetsov of the Kirov Ballet

Nina Ananiashvili of the Bolshoi Ballet and Otto Neubert of the New York City Ballet

this ballet to the Bolshoi, but it did not happen. Grigorovich did not want it so it didn't happen then. But we tried really hard. We talked with Peter [Martins] and it was really close but it did not happen. When Alexei Fadeyechev came to the theater, he brought Balanchine and the program to the Bolshoi. And I think our company danced really well. It was really a beautiful dance. 🙰

Nina Ananiashvili is one of today's finest international ballet stars. Schooled at the Bolshoi Ballet, she has made guest appearances with the Maryinsky Ballet, the New York City Ballet, the Royal Ballet, the Royal Danish Ballet, and American Ballet Theatre. She continues to perform around the world with her own troupe, Nina Ananiashvili and International Stars.

Veronika Part of the Kirov Ballet

Nina Ananiashvili and Andrei Uvarov of the Bolshoi Ballet

Ethan Stiefel

Albert Evans

Symphony in Three Movements

PREMIERE: JUNE 18, 1972
COMPANY: NEW YORK CITY BALLET
THEATER: NEW YORK STATE THEATER, NEW YORK

by Sara Leland

City Ballet's first Stravinsky Festival took place when *Symphony in Three Movements* was an incredible challenge for the company. I remember that the board agreed to our canceling all performances for the week before so we had extra time to rehearse the twenty-one new works and to fine-tune our eleven existing ballets to Stravinsky. Just imagine—seven nights with a different program every night! Yet despite all the pressure Mr. Balanchine must have been under, I cannot say that he worked any differently when preparing the festival. Yes, he was working very fast but then he always choreographed very fast, with whatever dancers were available at the time. Someone told me he once said, "I work like a dentist." I never heard him say that, but it is the truth.

The second movement pas de deux for Eddie Villella and me was made in only two days in two ninety-minute sessions. He described it as "Balinese" because of its undulating, snaky gestures. He occasionally used phrases to clarify a movement or step: "Hold the arms like a little window" or "Open like a flower." I believe he chose those Balinese movements to make good use of a lack of mine. I admit it: I had undisciplined, floppy hands and arms, so here he was getting the most out of what could be a drawback. Anyone else would choreograph to a dancer's strength, but Mr. Balanchine got results from a fault.

He did not insist on speed so much as on energy. There is a lot of prancing for the sixteen corps women in *Symphony.* And marching. I later learned that Stravinsky composed it during World War II and was reportedly influenced by the newsreels he saw. You can sense that influence in the first movement in the aggressive way the ten demi-soloists in black enter, with their elbows chugging away. You can hear it, too, in the tympani and brass of the movement that surrounds our little Balinese pas. Mr. Balanchine certainly heard it. Those slashing arm movements we make and the straight-arm poses we strike in the finale are called "The Salutes." I never thought I would be dancing in a ballet about Nazis or World War II.

I remember the Saturday evening rehearsal when the finale was being finished just before the opening-night gala when *Symphony* would be premiered. The counts are so tricky there—5 and 9 and 7 and 1-2-3—and some girls were actually crying and saying, "I'll never get it! I'll never get it!" Mr. Balanchine quietly announced that if we had to stay there all night, that was what we would do, but we would

finish the ballet that evening. His confidence and authority calmed everyone down, and we went back to work. Later there was an adjustment to the finale and a change in costumes, but the ballet was completed that night. ☙

Ethan Stiefel

Wendy Whelan

After studying with E. Virginia Williams of the New England Ballet, the predecessor of the Boston Ballet, and later discovered by Robert Joffrey, Sara Leland was seen at the Boston Ballet by George Balanchine, who invited her to become a member of the New York City Ballet. During her first year with the Company, she was given the leading role in Les Biches, a new ballet by Francisco Moncion. After becoming a soloist, she took on solo and principal roles in a variety of ballets, aided by her aptitude for learning parts quickly. She created roles in a number of works, including Don Quixote, Emeralds, Symphony in Three Movements, Union Jack, Vienna Waltzes, and Dances at a Gathering and the Goldberg Variations, as well as NYCB's 1967 revival of Frederick Ashton's Illuminations and the 1971 revival of Robbins' The Concert.

After having gradually assumed many of the duties of a ballet mistress, Miss Leland retired from performing in 1983 to devote herself full-time to the job of Assistant Ballet Mistress. With Bart Cook, she is responsible for the maintenance of much of the Robbins repertory, as well as some of Balanchine's work. She has staged works for companies in Holland, Cuba, and Denmark, as well as for the Joffrey Ballet, the Boston Ballet, and the Dance Theater of Harlem.

Sara Leland and Bart Cook

Kathleen Tracey and Kipling Houston

Ethan Stiefel

Diana Vishneva of the Kirov Ballet

Tchaikovsky Pas de Deux

PREMIERE: MARCH 29, 1960
COMPANY: NEW YORK CITY BALLET
THEATER: CITY CENTER OF MUSIC AND DRAMA, NEW YORK

By Cynthia Gregory

In my thirty-one years as a professional ballet dancer, I believe I danced in only nine Balanchine ballets. In just one of those pieces I was fortunate enough to work with George Balanchine himself. It was the glorious *Tchaikovsky Pas de Deux*.

Before I learned it, I had seen it danced by different dancers in different companies, but was particularly inspired by Violette Verdy in the role. Mr. Balanchine had used this music, originally written for *Swan Lake*, to create a very special pas de deux for Violette and her partner, Conrad Ludlow, in 1960. I must have seen them dance it in the late 1960s.

I was such a fan of Violette Verdy. She was exquisite—so musical, so vivacious, so utterly charming—absolutely dance personified! I only hoped I could do it justice, I thought, as I began to learn the steps of the pas de deux.

I had been invited along with Peter Martins to dance at a gala benefit performance honoring Norman Treigle, the New York City Opera star who had died the year before.

How great to dance with Peter again! We'd done a couple of guest performances together, and in many ways, he was my perfect partner. Tall, elegant, and handsome, he had a virtuosic technique and was the right size for me (a rather tall ballerina). I used to dream about him leaving the New York City Ballet and coming to dance with me at American Ballet Theatre as my regular partner. But Peter was committed to the New York City Ballet and to Balanchine. I couldn't blame him. So, therefore, I had to make do with guest performances here and there, now and then.

This one would be quite exciting. We'd be dancing in New York together for the first time and we'd be dancing the *Tchaikovsky Pas de Deux*. Peter thought that with a little luck, Mr. B might come to one of our rehearsals and coach us in it. Wanting to make the best impression I possibly could, I worked especially hard, concentrating on the qualities I knew Mr. B admired—sharp, quick footwork and musicality. The footwork speed was not my strongest suit, but I knew I was musical. It's why I danced—to describe the essence of the music.

One day, Peter and I were working in a New York State Theater rehearsal room when Mr. Balanchine showed up! We moved into the main rehearsal studio and began again. I felt so nervous sand so excited—like a beginning dancer rather than a seasoned ballerina from American Ballet Theatre .

Balanchine couldn't have been nicer. He watched, he corrected, he demonstrated, he even changed a few things to suit my way of dancing. Then he wished us luck and was gone. It was my one special hour working with George Balanchine.

A few days later, our performance of the *Tchaikovsky Pas de Deux* went very well. Afterwards, Peter told me "You know, Cynthia, Mr. B really liked you. He said 'She dances fast for a girl from ABT.'"

That was a compliment, indeed. 🙶

Cynthia Gregory, whom Rudolf Nureyev called "America's prima ballerina assoluta," was celebrated as one of the greatest dancers of her era during a career that spanned more than thirty years. She danced with San Francisco Ballet, American Ballet Theatre, and as a guest artist with leading ballet companies around the world. Now a busy wife and mother, she coaches, stages the classics, and interprets some of her most memorable roles in pen-and-ink and watercolor drawings.

Mr. Balanchine rehearses Patricia McBride and Mikhail Baryshnikov

Damian Woetzel

Diana Vishneva of the Kirov Ballet

Diana Vishneva of the Kirov Ballet

Merrill Ashley

Tchaikovsky Piano Concerto #2

PREMIERE: JUNE 25, 1941
COMPANY: AMERICAN BALLET CARAVAN
THEATER: TEATRO MUNICIPAL, RIO DE JANIERO, BRAZIL

by Robert Gottlieb

Both the name and the look of *Ballet Imperial* have changed continually since it first was created for American Ballet Caravan's 1941 tour of South America, something cooked up by Lincoln Kirstein and Nelson Rockefeller, who was then in the Latin-American division of the State Department. The premiere took place in Rio de Janeiro in June (an open dress rehearsal had been held in New York a month earlier); it was performed briefly in New York late in 1942; and it entered the New York City Ballet repertory in 1964 (featuring Suzanne Farrell and Jacques d'Amboise). By the time it was revived in a new production in 1973 (featuring Patricia McBride and Peter Martins), it had become *Concerto No. 2,* and the ornate Rouben Ter-Arutunian sets and costumes had been banished. Classical tutus were replaced by soft chiffon dresses by Karinska, there was no pictorial background, no views of the Maryinsky and the Neva, and there were changes to the choreography, particularly in the second movement. In the 1980s, the costumes changed again, and now it was being called *Tchaikovsky Piano Concerto No. 2,* whereas at American Ballet Theatre in the 1990s, it was back to being called *Ballet Imperial,* and it once again had an ornate set and formal tutus.

Even though you can do away with the St. Petersburg decor and the classical costumes, you cannot disguise the opulence, the grandeur, and the difficulties of the choreography. From the start, it was recognized how demanding the first movement was for the ballerina—except that Balanchine's first American-trained ballerina, Marie-Jeanne, for whom *Ballet Imperial* (as well as *Concerto Barocco*) was made, apparently had no technical weaknesses; everyone reported on her lightning jumps and steely

Merrill Ashley and Sean Lavery

pointes. She needed them: even Merrill Ashley, whose speed and precision are legendary, uses phrases like "notoriously difficult" and "monumental difficulty" when describing this first movement in her memoirs. But going beyond the technical demands, she also rightly stresses the imperial, almost imperious, quality Balanchine required of the ballerina in this role, whether the word "imperial" appeared in the title or not. When she circles the stage at the start, he told Ashley, she must barely acknowledge "her subjects," the corps. "Don't look at them!" he said. "Don't acknowledge them! You're royalty. Royalty doesn't have to bow to anyone. They bow to you and you ignore them."

Only the most technically advanced ballerinas attempt this role. Even as great a dancer as Margot Fonteyn found it not only daunting but also unachievable when Balanchine set it on the Royal Ballet. She told me once, "I used to stand in the wings at the beginning, waiting for my entrance and thinking that if I could just get through that first passage I'd be all right. But you know, Bob, I never could. Moira [Shearer] was a lot better!" (a judgment confirmed to me by Balanchine himself).

But *Ballet Imperial* goes beyond the rigorous demands of the first movement. The plangent second movement, with the new duet Balanchine made for the 1973 version, has echoes of *Swan Lake* in much the way *Theme and Variations* comments on *The Sleeping Beauty*. And the intricate weavings of its corps girls as they fan out from the male principal in convoluted chains and then spiral back in again are probably the most elaborate Balanchine ever invented. (On one terrifying occasion at the New York State Theater, I saw the two lines of eight girls each get muddled; it was like a pile-up in a mass traffic accident.) Then—bam!—with no

Robert Tewsley   *Miranda Weese and Robert Tewsley*

pause, as the principals exit, the third movement slams onto the stage and one of Balanchine's most exciting finales starts to build. This is pure kinetic excitement and glamour, resolving the glittering coolness of the first movement and the deep feeling of the second.

For me, more even than *Theme and Variations* and *Diamonds,* this ballet is Balanchine's fullest statement about Tchaikovsky, Petipa, and classicism. I think I may find it so moving because in some way, as it follows the structure of Tchaikovsky's very extended and very grand concerto, it affects me the way certain great novels do. We follow one dominant couple throughout the entire ballet, as opposed to the four couples of *Symphony in C,* say, or the two couples that split the honors in *Stravinsky Violin Concerto.* (There are subsidiary dramas for the second ballerina and her two escorts—big novels need secondary characters to help create an entire world—but the trajectory of the imperial pair remains our focus.) Not that Balanchine intended any kind of story, but in obedience to the music, he created a dramatic action that carries through three large territories.

That *Ballet Imperial* may be performed less frequently than some other Balanchine classical ballets is less a comment on its quality than a reflection of its demands. In tutus or tunics, danced against a palace ballroom or a simple cyclorama, it requires both superlative technique and consummate grandeur.

Robert Gottlieb has been editor-in-chief of Alfred A. Knopf and of The New Yorker. *He served for many years on the board of directors of New York City Ballet and is currently the dance critic of the* New York Observer.

Robert Tewsley

Ib Andersen

Theme and Variations

Premiere: November 26, 1947
Company: Ballet Theatre
Theater: City Center of Music and Drama, New York

by Olga Chenchikova

The year 1989 was a very important one for me. That was the year when my daughter, Masha, was born, and that was the year when, having returned to the company [Kirov Ballet] a year before, I danced *Theme and Variations*, and thus one of the greatest choreographers in history, George Balanchine, came into my artistic life. I was deeply impressed by the premiere at our theater and I looked very much forward to rehearsing this ballet.

Theme and Variations is a ballet with refined and solemn ceremonial dances. Precisely marked and finely drawn choreographic bars saturate technical and emotional potential. Only a highly professional company can afford having Balanchine in its repertory, and this ballet had become, in a certain way, a test not only for me, but also for the whole company. The virtuosic choreography demands a brilliant corps de ballet, and the company performed this ballet to the highest standards.

Everything in this ballet is very logical for me— intonation, rhythm, and musicality. It is musicality in the first place that stirs up my admiration. I would like to recall the conductor of this performance, Dzemal Dalgat. He was an extraordinary musician with a delicate perception of music and an extraordinary gift for understanding the musical and choreographic text of this ballet.

Merrill Ashley

Faruk Ruzimatov of the Kirov Ballet

The unique choice of music allowed Balanchine to create depth in his artistic images. There is nothing extra in this ballet—movement and music mesh to create a pure harmony, captured in Balanchine's choreography.

I was partnered with Makhar Vaziev. We were creating a fragile world where subtle half-glances would reveal a versatile emotional background, whether being constructed through inner interaction or directly with the public. That world would take us to our future with its joys and hopes.

It is amazing how Balanchine would open up all the facets of the personality of each particular ballerina, her talent, and her individuality. He makes us admire and worship a ballerina, making her the central point in his choreography. His ballets truly respond to the artistic conception of the Russian ballerinas, with their mentality and ability to feel and hear music. It is not by chance that I chose

Jean-Pierre Bonnefoux

Faruk Ruzimatov of the Kirov Ballet

to perform this particular ballet on my recital evening, as this choreography could reveal my feelings and heart like no other.

Today I pass my love and admiration for Balanchine on to my students. I tell them, "Music will give you the true feeling of movement and images of this ballet. Listen to the music and Balanchine will teach you how to dance." ✒

Olga Chenchikova's dance career began with a silver medal at the Moscow International Ballet Competition in 1973. She immediately was accepted into the bllet company of the Perm Theater and, after a 1977 guest performance at the Maryinsky Theater, was invited to join the company. During her time at the Maryinsky, she became one of the company's most well-known performers, dancing the principal roles in many classic and contemporary ballets. After a major injury in 1995, she left the stage and became a senior repetiteur at the Maryinsky.

Ethan Stiefel

Tamara Rojo of the Royal Ballet (U.K.) rehearses

New York City Ballet

Le Tombeau de Couperin

PREMIERE: MAY 29, 1975
COMPANY: NEW YORK CITY BALLET
THEATER: RAVEL FESTIVAL, NEW YORK STATE THEATER, NEW YORK

by Rosemary Dunleavy

New York City Ballet's 1975 Ravel Festival consisted almost entirely of world premieres. In two and a half weeks, sixteen ballets were performed, and Mr. B provided more than half the repertory—eight new works plus his 1951 masterpiece, *La Valse.* His contributions ranged from a solo (Pavane) and a pas de deux (Sonatine) to a one-act opera in which dancers represented crockery, furniture, and animals (*L'Enfant et les Sortilèges,* premiered by Diaghilev's Ballets Russes in 1925 in Balanchine's staging). Unusual as *L'Enfant* was for City Ballet, it was not the only novelty offered during the festival. *Le Tombeau de Couperin,* set to the

four-movement orchestral version of Ravel's six-part 1919 piano suite, was that Balanchine rarity, a work created entirely for the corps de ballet with no solos. It was the first work created for the festival, choreographed by Mr. B well in advance and then set aside. When the company began to concentrate on the other works to be premiered, the dancers and I got together and reassembled it, so to speak. We then asked Mr. B to take enough time off from his festival duties to look at it again. He watched us perform it in the studio. When we finished, he said, "You know, I like it. It's a good ballet."

Tombeau was a classic example of Balanchine's inventive and continuously shifting floor patterns, in this case for eight couples, which must have made it a particular favorite of subscribers up in the New York State Theater's Fourth Ring. These patterns could be described as "kaleidoscopic," since there were few symmetrical, or "mirror," images in which Couple A, say, and Couple E would face each other while performing the same steps or gestures simultaneously or in canonic sequence. In *Tombeau,* it was as if Balanchine had drawn a line diagonally through the stage; Couple A would be at upstage right

New York City Ballet

and Couple E at downstage left. He regularly worked variations on this arrangement to keep the stage picture constantly refreshed.

The sixteen dancers were divided into a Left Quadrille (danced at the premiere by Judith Fugate and Jean-Pierre Frohlich, Wilhelmina Frankfurt and Victor Castelli, Muriel Aasen and Francis Sackett, and Susan Hendl and David Richardson) and a Right Quadrille (Marjorie Spohn and Hermes Condé, Delia Peters and Richard Hoskinson, Susan Pilarre and Richard Dryden, and Carol Sumner and Laurence Matthews). The opening of the Prelude—all eight couples onstage standing apart in a great circle—was atypically symmetrical. Although dancers were listed in pairs in the program, these "partnerships" did not last long, for the women soon left the men to dance with other partners and remained with them. The partnering in this movement was very courtly, with the men bowing to the women at its conclusion.

New York City Ballet

The rhythm was more stately in Forlane, the following movement, and the dancers tended to move in groups of four. A pas de quatre would involve an interlacing of arms or a couple crossing underneath another's upraised arms. Four by four they would often come together to form the letter "M" upstage.

There is no better demonstration of the uniqueness of *Tombeau* among Balanchine ballets than the fact that the partnering contains no soaring lifts until the third movement, Menuet, and then these involve only half the couples. Typically, Balanchine saved the lifts for the trio, or midpoint of the piece, when there was a gentle upsurge in the music. (Ravel's rhythm throughout is subtler than the more pronounced beat of the classical minuet.) As an added subtlety, the lifts were also done at the midpoint of the stage among the corps, not down toward the footlights. The dancers resumed the steps of the opening when its music returned.

The finale, Rigaudon, was the liveliest movement of the four, with some fleeting, polka-style partnering. At another point the men even stood with their feet crossed or rocked back and forth on their heels. The mood and the stage picture changed completely with the gently lilting B melody. A diagonal corridor was formed, with all eight women kneeling on one side and all eight men kneeling on the other, and couples came forward to dance in the cleared space. The return of the A melody found everyone in high spirits, with handclaps and handshakes among the men. *Tombeau* concluded with eight couples facing out into the house once more.

Rosemary Dunleavy joined the New York City Ballet in 1961 and performed in almost every ballet in the company's repertory. In 1971, she retired from dancing to become George Balanchine's full-time Assistant Ballet Mistress. She was promoted to Ballet Mistress in 1983 and is responsible for the vast majority of the Balanchine works in the repertory.

New York City Ballet

New York City Ballet

Suzanne Farrell

Tzigane

PREMIERE: MAY 29, 1975
COMPANY: NEW YORK CITY BALLET
THEATER: RAVEL FESTIVAL, NEW YORK STATE THEATER, NEW YORK

By Sarah Kaufman

Gypsies have been a tantalizing ballet subject since the early 1800s, when archrivals Marie Taglioni and Fanny Elssler starred as gypsies in separate vehicles. Then, as for George Balanchine in 1975, a ballerina throwing herself into a gypsy dance was a singularly alluring creature, at once virgin and vamp, part elegant aristocrat and part dangerous Other.

However, Balanchine's *Tzigane,* set to Maurice Ravel's score of the same name, is a more loaded gypsy dance. It was the first ballet he created for Suzanne Farrell following their six-year rupture. With it, the choreographer paid tribute to the grown-up, more worldly and knowing dancer.

This ballet is not about a vision, an untouchable love object or notions of perfection. This ballet is about a woman.

The moon is full; the trees are clipped, stylized. A dancer saunters slowly into the light. Her bodice is cut low and her skirt has been slashed into shreds of red fabric. Her hair is tied in a ponytail, which whips around like the ribbony strands of her frock when she dances. She is in a natural, undone state, wild and unharnessed, like the movement that boils out of her.

Abrupt, passionate, and brashly dramatic dancing matches the intricacies and flourishes of Ravel's solo violin cadenza. At times the dancer thrusts her hands forward as if she is tearing something out of her breast. At other times her arms soften and melt, as if in surrender. Her fingers, wrists, and shoulders are electrified; she dips into a deep backbend and her arms snake into the air above her exposed neck.

Her legs kick and lunge, rotate inward, and fly into the air, pulling her across the stage in hungry bursts. There is something desperate and imperative in her movement. The dance is a necessity, and the burning emotional force of it pulls us close.

The entire ballet is scarcely ten minutes long, and fully half of that is the ballerina's solo—one woman, one instrument. So simple, and yet infinitely resonant. The movement here is unlike any other Balanchine work. As Ravel was inspired by Gypsy fiddling, Balanchine riffs on Hungarian-flavored folk dance. The melancholy and the hot feelings are there, with suggestions of boots and *czardas* steps and even palmistry. But he creates a whole new language of long, slicing lines, broken edges, undulating currents, and sudden pops, like sparks bursting from embers.

Mr. Balanchine rehearses

Peter Martins

A man appears in the background—Peter Martins, in the original cast. He inches closer, captivated by the woman and trying to mirror her movements, but we know he will fail to possess her.

As the orchestra joins in, the dancing takes on a more pronounced folk feel, with four other couples forming a stamping, spinning backdrop. It is Balanchine's genius that the movement that had seemed so personal to the star—to Farrell—has now been retooled into a group exercise of exultant force.

But the focus remains on the woman, and on the man who follows her as if drawn into a whirlpool. They dance together for a few moments, then she spins away. In the end, all he can do is fall on one knee in deference to her mystery.

Suzanne Farrell

There is nothing coolly classical about *Tzigane*. Brief as it is, it is a stage-filling drama, seething with feeling. And it brilliantly, imaginatively expressed the new relationship between the choreographer and his muse. Balanchine celebrates Farrell's wildness and her spirit, recognizing that she has returned to his camp and continues to surprise and sustain him, but she cannot truly be claimed. 🌿

Sarah Kaufman has been the chief dance critic of The Washington Post *since 1996. She has been writing on dance for two decades. She has received awards for both her criticism and feature writing, and frequently lectures on journalism. She lives in Maryland with her husband and three children.*

Suzanne Farrell

Peter Martins

New York City Ballet

Union Jack

PREMIERE: MAY 13, 1976
COMPANY: NEW YORK CITY BALLET
THEATER: NEW YORK STATE THEATER, NEW YORK

By Richard N. Philp

The year is 1976, and the United States has, after years of preparation, launched itself full guns into the bicentennial celebration of the signing of the Declaration of Independence in 1776. While the nation sponsors explosions of red, white, and blue, New York City Ballet has devised what will become one of its most successful full-company spectacles, the three-part ballet *Union Jack*. This is an elaborate seventy-minute-long panegyric—*not* about the anniversary of the start of the American Revolution, but celebrating our eighteenth-century English *oppressors,* against whom the eight-year war for independence was fought in the first place. It is, well, an odd choice, perhaps among the oddest in that year of bicentennial commemorations. But the rather spectacular results soon sweep aside any initial questions about appropriateness.

For the bicentennial, Balanchine really could not produce another *Stars and Stripes* (1958), an immensely popular, if ironic, work satirizing the excessive patriotism encountered in America during the decade following World War II. And, as things turned out, Balanchine wanted to link the American *Stars and Stripes*, the British *Union Jack*, and the far less successful Francophile *Tricolore* (1978) into a full evening, to which he gave the hopeful working title *Entente Cordiale*. He was heartily encouraged to choreograph *Union Jack* by Lincoln Kirstein (according to Kirstein's own account), who was an unrepentant Anglophile, a man with a more than passing fancy for all things having to do with the English. The reasons for this approach, at least in Kirstein's corner, are

New York City Ballet

undoubtedly complex. But Balanchine's attractions to the British topic seem far more direct and simpler. *Scotch Symphony* (1952) marked his first use of kilts and Scottish folk dance forms in a ballet, and he wanted to explore the subject further. During the five summer seasons in the 1920s that he had spent working in London with Diaghilev's Ballets Russes, he had immersed himself in London's music-hall traditions, which fascinated him, as he would later immerse himself in Broadway and American films.

The official premiere of *Union Jack* ("Union Jack" is slang for the British national flag) had décor and costumes by the perennial Rouben Ter-Arutunian. Hershy Kay wrote a score based on British music-hall songs, regimental music, and folk dance tunes, most notably the hornpipe. Kay writes that Balanchine had asked him to create "in essence, a British *Stars and Stripes.*"

The ballet is in three sections. The stunning opening of the first section begins with what appears to be knife-edged, mathematical precision to Scottish regimental drum music, which introduces seven clans, three of male dancers, four of female. This is followed by a series of classical variations for seventy dancers in teams of ten.

The second section is an extended pas de deux, in the manner of what you might expect to find in a husband-and-wife star-turn in London music halls a century ago. That the real-life husband-and-wife team of Jean-Pierre Bonnefoux and Patricia McBride danced the original Pearly King and Pearly Queen added another inside dimension worth close watching.

The final section, with nautical tunes and setting, makes use of the hornpipe in complex variations that require extended virtuoso dancing. And—just as we might have suspected from the very beginning—down comes an enormous Union Jack covering the back stage wall. As a sort of coda, the entire company, to the stir-

New York City Ballet

New York City Ballet

ring tune of "Rule Britannia," signals with red and yellow semaphore flags the words "God Save the Queen."

A ballet that requires many dancers, *Union Jack* might come across today as more than a mere celebration of the residue of British history on American culture. In the context of one of the most powerful alliances in modern times, you may leave the theater humming tunes, yes, but also thinking about what they have come to mean in a much larger—or perhaps much *smaller*—world. Anyway, I do. ✍

Mr. Balanchine's curtain call after premiere

Richard Philp is, after thirty-three years in dance journalism, Editor-in-Chief emeritus of Dance Magazine, *where his monthly column of commentary, "Kickoff," ran from 1989 through 2002. Lecturer, consultant, and writer, his most recent work,* Romeos Dancing, Shakespeare Without Words, *is published by Micawber Press.*

Mr. Balanchine and the company celebrate at the end of the premiere of Union Jack

Wendy Whelan and New York City Ballet

New York City Ballet

La Valse

PREMIERED FEBRUARY 20, 1951
COMPANY: NEW YORK CITY BALLET
THEATER: CITY CENTER OF MUSIC AND DRAMA, NEW YORK

by Harris Green

Maurice Ravel's *Valses Nobles et Sentimentales* and *La Valse* had been used by choreographers before Balanchine combined the two works for New York City Ballet in 1951 as *La Valse*. Both scores were originally written for piano. *Vienna* (1907), a glorification of Schubert and Johann Strauss, was orchestrated by Ravel in 1920 at Diaghilev's urging and retitled *La Valse*. Now "a choreographic poem for orchestra" and a bitter reflection on the chaos of World War I, the brooding, volcanic score was rejected by Diaghilev. Bronislava Nijinska's version for Ida Rubinstein's company was premiered at the Paris Opera in 1929. *Valses Nobles et Sentimentales*, composed in 1911 as a set of eight Schubertian piano pieces, was orchestrated in 1912 for a recital by Russian ballerina Natasha Trouhanova. Nineteen-year-old Georgi Melitonovich Balanchivadze (later George Balanchine) choreographed one of the waltzes for the Petrograd avant-garde troupe Young Ballet in 1923.

Balanchine's gothic scenario for *La Valse*, with its shattering conclusion, was possibly suggested by Edgar Allan Poe's 1842 short story, "The Masque of the Red Death." *Valses Nobles et Sentimentales* opens the work, with the first waltz played as an overture. The second instantly sets a pervading mood of elegance and menace. Three mysterious women are discovered onstage. (You are free to call them the Fates if you wish; Balanchine assigned names to no one.) They wear long white gloves and ankle-length Romantic tutus of tulle and net, layered in rose and gray—one of Karinska's more striking inspirations. Instead of dancing, they gesture with flexed wrists and arms upraised. Each of the next three waltzes is danced by a different formally dressed couple. The three women return to claim the man of the third for the seventh

and most impassioned waltz—his partner had danced the sixth as a solo—in which a main theme of *La Valse* receives a vigorous statement.

The eighth and last waltz, a gentle descent into silence, provides a haunting accompaniment for the

meeting of The Girl and her partner. A vision of innocence clad entirely in white, she enters with arms stretched out as in yearning, only to be seemingly blown back. Her partner meets her at center stage for a "conversation" in gestures similar to those of the mysterious trio. The figure of Death is revealed

Jennie Taylor and Sebastien Marcovici

watching them as the couple exits (an addition Balanchine made in 1974).

As the music of *La Valse* begins, Balanchine approximates the description Ravel provided in the score ("[C]louds . . . part to reveal a glimpse of waltzing couples. . . . The stage gradually brightens. The glow of the chandeliers breaks out fortissimo"). Individual members of the three couples cross and recross the darkened stage. One man pauses in a spotlight to stare into the dark. The light sweeps from him to reveal the enigmatic trio standing ominously still. (Complimented on this inspiration, lighting designer Jean Rosenthal said, "It was Mr. Balanchine's idea.") When fully revealed, the ballroom—suggested by fabric arches hanging upstage—is thronged with a corps of sixteen women, nine men, and the previous couples, waltzing or performing variants of the waltz. At the peak of their exuberance, The Girl and her partner cross the stage in grands jetés.

As the music begins to throb to the rhythm of a heartbeat, the dancers freeze in a *tableau vivant*, and Death and his attendant approach, drawing The Girl to them as in a swoon. From a tray held by

Louise Nadeau of Pacific Northwest Ballet

the attendant, Death takes a set of gifts entirely in black: earrings, a necklace, a belted mesh overdress, mesh gloves (donned to a chilling downward spiral in the orchestra), and a bouquet that she suddenly finds repulsive. Seeing her reflection in the cracked mirrored surface of the tray, she recoils but is powerless to resist Death's partnering her in a violent, fatal waltz. He lets her body fall to the floor and withdraws. Her partner, with her corpse in his arms, wanders abjectly among the now animated and indifferent corps. The men take the body from him and hold it aloft in the center of a wildly circling corps ("a fantastic and fatefully inescapable whirlpool") as the curtain falls.

No discussion of *La Valse* would be complete without mention of Tanaquil Le Clercq, whose haunting performance as the doomed heroine was considered definitive. While a teenager at the School of American Ballet, she had played a girl stricken with polio in *Resurgence*, a January 1946 *pièce d'occasion* created by Balanchine for a March of Dimes benefit at the Waldorf-Astoria. On tour with NYCB in October 1956, Le Clercq contracted polio in Copenhagen and never danced again. ❧

Harris Green is a former features editor of Dance Magazine *who has written about the performing arts for* The New Republic, Ballet Review, *and* The New York Times.

The Fates as played by members of the New York City Ballet

New York City Ballet

Peter Boal

Vienna Waltzes

PREMIERE: JUNE 23, 1977
COMPANY: NEW YORK CITY BALLET
THEATER: NEW YORK STATE THEATER, NEW YORK

by Sean Lavery

While he was working on *Vienna Waltzes*, Mr. Balanchine would take all of us to the main hall and make sure that every couple was rehearsed in the proper way to waltz. He was very specific about the style. You do not go up and down, but glide. The weight had to be on the man's right hand so the effect would be light. You had to hold the woman's arms just so and she had to hold her head the correct way. He was adamant about these matters. It is incredible when you think of it, how there is nothing but waltzing or variations of waltzing in every movement except the third, but you never get bored with the form.

The first part, set to Johann Strauss's "Tales from the Vienna Woods," sets everything up. It has the most waltzing and having to choreograph around designer Rouben Ter-Arutunian's "forest" was a challenge Mr. Balanchine met with constantly interesting patterns, sometimes for ten corps couples, sometimes just for the women. It was my introduction to working with Mr. Balanchine as he choreographed. I was new to the company, having made my debut that season as Titania's cavalier in *A Midsummer Night's Dream*. Two days before the preview at the spring gala, he pulled me out of the corps to replace an injured Jacques d'Amboise as Karin von Aroldingen's partner. He was still at work on

the ending, when the main theme of the waltz comes rushing back. Would Karin and I suddenly go whirling off into the wings? Most choreographers would have had us do something predictable like that. Mr. Balanchine decided to have us simply walk off as we had entered, slowly arm in arm.

In the second movement, set to Strauss's The Voices of Spring and involving few trees, the women are costumed like woodsy sprites and the two principals never waltz together. There are waltz positions throughout, however, as when the woman does an attitude.

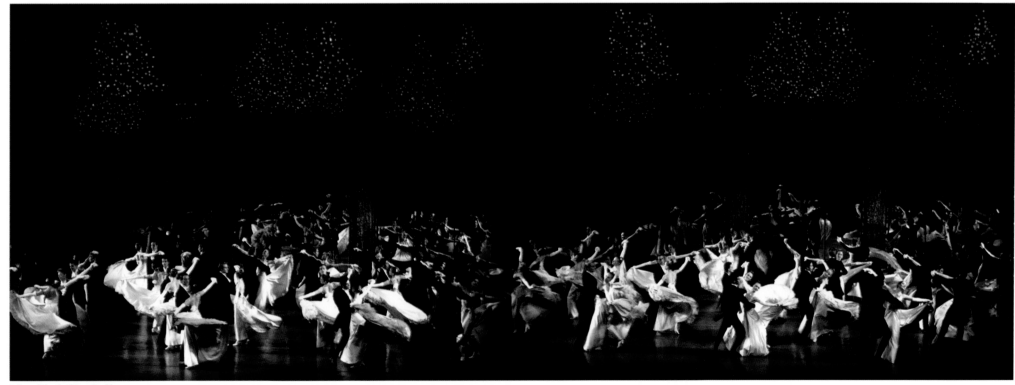

New York City Ballet

Mr. Balanchine gives some final words of advice to a dancer before the curtain is raised

Since it is set to Strauss's "Explosion Polka" instead of a waltz, the third movement is not like any other section of *Vienna Waltzes*. It is broad, raucous, vulgar, and flat-footed, with the guys in grotesque wigs and striped pants. Mr. Balanchine obviously wanted a contrast at this point and he certainly got it. The first major scenery change occurs here in the third movement, the setting transforms from a woodland setting to a gay '90s café with a floor for waltzing. I am told that Ter-Arutunian got the idea for the transformation when he realized that the period's undulating, entwining decorative styles resembled tree roots. As the forest backdrop is slowly pulled up, the ensnarled roots become the urban setting. Now it is just a matter of carrying on some tables and chairs and the scene is set for The Officer—or is he a Count?—to meet The Lady in Black.

You would not think it to look at it because the action is so straightforward but the fourth movement ("Merry Widow"), set to Franz Lehár's "The Gold and Silver Waltz," gave Mr. Balanchine a great deal of trouble. He could not decide on the ending and kept going back to it after *Vienna Waltzes* had entered the repertory. Would she run out and leave him alone? Would they leave together? Would they be left alone onstage? Would they be together onstage in silhouette? He settled on the last one.

Suzanne Farrell of the New York City Ballet and Jorge Donn of the Bejart Ballet of the 20th Century

Karin von Aroldingen

The final movement, to a suite from Richard Strauss's *Der Rosenkavalier*, offered another example of Mr. Balanchine's efficiency under pressure. He was still working on the ending of the big waltz right up to an hour of so before the preview. At that point, the five main couples were waltzing in the center, surrounded by the corps. I remember he looked at his watch and saw it was five to six. He thought about how much music was left to choreograph. Then he said, "Okay, everyone stop and walk forward. You open up. You go over there. You go over there." Later on the tour in Washington, D.C., he changed the entrance of the principals, but that is how *Vienna Waltzes* ended. ✍

Sean Lavery began his ballet training in his hometown of Harrisburg, Pennsylvania, at the age of ten. As a Principal Dancer with the New York City Ballet, Mr. Lavery originated roles in numerous ballets. In addition to his duties as Assistant to the Ballet Master-in-Chief for New York City Ballet, Mr. Lavery stages Balanchine ballets for the George Balanchine Trust and is a teaching assistant for both the School of American Ballet and the New York City Ballet.

Suzanne Farrell

Karin von Aroldingen and Sean Lavery

Kyra Nichols and Ben Huys

Walpurgisnacht

Premiere: May 15, 1980
Company: New York City Ballet
Theater: New York State Theater, New York

By Don McDonagh

Almost from the beginning of his career outside Russia in 1925, Balanchine found himself confronted with various pieces of *musique dansante* composed by Gounod for the opera *Faust*. "Can you work quickly?" asked impresario Serge Diaghilev, and then assigned his newly employed young choreographer the task of preparing suitable ballets for eight other operas as well

during the Spring Monte Carlo residence of his Ballets Russes company. The demonstration of Balanchine's skilled facility prompted Diaghilev to designate him as his chief choreographer, a position Balanchine held until the dissolution of the company after Diaghilev's death in 1929.

Fifty years later, in 1975, Balanchine choreographed the *Walpurgisnacht Ballet* for the Paris Opéra's production of *Faust*. In 1980 it became an independent work in the repertory of the New York City Ballet. It calls for two principals, one woman and one man, three female solo dancers, and twenty corps de ballet women.

Mr. Balanchine instructs the cast while Rosemary Dunleavy looks on

Suzanne Farrell and Adam Lüders

The ballet is without a specific program but places the only male in the midst of a maelstrom of energetic women who form an increasingly agitated vortex around him. They move from a jaunty and wicked faun prance to an excited running that is emphasized by their wildly streaming hair, loosened from its original tied-back restraint. At one point they all leave the stage to the man who crosses it diagonally to the accompaniment of a somewhat longing melody emerging from the background of insistent, urging music. From among the crowd of women surging back on the stage, he lifts and displays the principal woman overhead exultantly as the others line up in a pyramid formation spreading out from the couple, confirming their prominence.

The ballet amusingly suggests the hyper-charged atmosphere of disciplined eroticism on public display that surrounded the Paris Opéra in the nineteenth-century heyday of its cultural influence throughout the European ballet world. The rhythmic excess of the score is beautifully reflected in this affectionate and lightly parodied expression of that fever.

Don McDonagh is an author and critic who has reviewed dance performances for a variety of publications during the past four decades; among them are The New York Times, Dance Magazine, *and* Ballet Review. *He has contributed articles to a variety of scholarly publications including the* International Encyclopedia of Dance *and the* Dictionary of American Biography. *His books include* George Balanchine (*a critical monograph*), How to Enjoy Ballet, Martha Graham (*a biography*), *and* The Rise and Fall and Rise of Modern Dance (*a critical history*).

Suzanne Farrell and Joseph Duell

Albert Evans and members of New York City Ballet

Western Symphony

PREMIERE: SEPTEMBER 7, 1954
COMPANY: NEW YORK CITY BALLET
THEATER: CITY CENTER OF MUSIC AND DRAMA, NEW YORK

by Martha Ullman West

Miss Kitty in a tutu, arms rippling like a swan queen's . . . John Wayne in spangled boots, strumming on his hat. For nearly half a century dancers clothed in Karinska's elegantly vulgar *Western Symphony* costumes have conjured up those small- and large-screen images whenever and wherever the ballet has been performed. Call it a horse ballet or even a *pirozhki* western, against a backdrop that looks like the set of a grade B movie, accompanied by music that at best is sentimental and at worst corny, Balanchine has created exuberant, witty dancing in a sophisticated take on the American West disseminated by popular culture.

Western Symphony opens with a waggle of dance hall girls in ruched tutus joined by cowpokes in a square dance of do-si-dos and pas de chat. It ends with the curtain descending on thirty-two dancers, whooping like rodeo competitors while they whip through multiple pirouettes en masse. In between are three sections of solos, pas de deux, and small ensemble dances that could be right at home in any full-length Russian story ballet.

The scope for shtick is broad and there are killingly funny moments: Pacific Northwest Ballet's Julie Tobiason, batting her eyes at her cowboy lover as she emerges from a fish dive; Tanaquil Le Clercq's strutting on pointe beneath a hat that Lillie Langtry might have worn (possibly the smartest chapeau in ballet). The use of costumes is a major part of the wit: in this ballet, Balanchine and Karinska proved themselves the masters of the flounce.

Like many Europeans of his generation, Balanchine adored the idea of the American West. "If you were to say to me, 'What's the best thing in America, artistically the best thing?'" he told a biographer, "I would reply 'Cowboys! Westerns!' The people are right for it, they know how to do what they're doing and to me it all rings true." ⁓

Martha Ullman West is a senior advisory editor at Dance Magazine, *for which she has been covering dance in Oregon and elsewhere as a correspondent and critic since 1980. She grew up in New York, attending performances at New York City Ballet from its beginning in 1948.*

Valentina Kozlova and Lindsay Fischer

Sofiane Sylve of the National Ballet of the Netherlands

Maria Kowroski and members of New York City Ballet

left and right: Robert La Fosse performs a solo

Who Cares?

PREMIERE: FEBRUARY 5, 1970
COMPANY: NEW YORK CITY BALLET
THEATER: NEW YORK STATE THEATER, NEW YORK

By Larry Kaplan

Created in 1970 during what is generally considered a fallow period for Balanchine, *Who Cares?* has become one of his most popular beloved works. Hershy Kay orchestrated the music for the music for the ballet, according to Gershwin's own piano arrangements. The setting is a stylized New York City skyline that suggests high-class glamour and the idealized romance of a bygone era.

Balanchine was personally acquainted with Gershwin. He worked with him in Hollywood on the *Goldwyn Follies*, and *Who Cares?* resonates with attributes usually associated with the composer: urbanity, sophistication, romance, charm, and serious musical intelligence. Alongside Gershwin's exuberant music, the rollicking orchestrations, and the sense of show business that informs the ballet, Balanchine's choreography is dense and concentrated. It dwells on the structure of the songs, and matches them with strict classical movement that expresses a surprisingly wide range of emotions—tenderness, passion, youthful high spirits, nonchalance, optimism, headstrong independence, sexual delight, and outright joy.

A long introductory section for an ensemble of a female corps and five soloist couples performing a succession of variations and pas de deux jampacked with steps sets the stage for the ballet's second half, which is its heart. Here a leading male dancer performs with three ballerinas, alternately invoking a Broadway/Hollywood hoofer in the manner of Fred Astaire and Gene Kelly and a young god of classical ballet dancing with the muses. The writer Robert Sealy once described the two sections of the ballet as *Raymonda on Fifth Avenue* and *Apollo in Central Park*.

Jacques d'Amboise created the leading male role, and the ballet presented him with one of his greatest triumphs. His ballerinas were Patricia McBride, Karin von Aroldingen, and Marnee Morris, each of whom suggested a different sort of romantic temperament. *Who Cares?* hits a high straightaway in the second section that it never tops with the exquisite pas de deux danced by d'Amboise and McBride to "The Man I Love" which evokes the deepest feelings of tenderness and romance. The choreography, with its intricate partnering movements that keep the ballerina off balance, seemed to grow out of the material Balanchine developed for McBride in *Rubies*, transforming Stravinsky's strutting filly from that ballet into Gershwin's more emotionally dependent and pliant damsel.

Patricia McBride

Monique Meunier and Nikolaj Hübbe

The material for the other principal women reflects their individual talents, too. Von Aroldingen's juicy Amazonian jumps in "Stairway to Paradise" and Marnee Morris's powerfully vertiginous turns in "My One and Only" define the roles and make them richly satisfying. Morris and Von Aroldgingen made indelible impressions, and, as happens so often with Balanchine ballets, it is practically impossible for those who saw them to imagine anyone but the original cast dancing the ballet. Yet succeeding generations of NYCB dancers have made their mark in *Who Cares?*—one thinks of Sean Lavery in the d'Amboise role, Kyra Nichols in Von Aroldingen's, Merrill Ashley in Morris's.

Wendy Whelan

Over the years, however, although nearly every NYCB principal ballerina has tried her hand at dancing "The Man I Love," no one has measured up to McBride. They have not even come close. It appears that she is irreplaceable in the role. Balanchine captured the essence of McBride in the choreography; her melancholy, poetic, romantic, playful, technically accomplished interpretation haunts the ballet with a beauty and magic that seem to shine down on it today. ❦

Merrill Ashley

Jacques d'Amboise and Marnee Morris

Larry Kaplan writes frequently for Ballet Review. *He has assisted in biographies of Merrill Ashley, Edward Villella, and Maria Tallchief.*

Maria Tallchief rehearses Judith Fugate in Sylvia Pas de Deux

The George Balanchine Foundation

By Nancy Reynolds

Whenever people ask me—as they frequently do—what is the difference between The George Balanchine Foundation and The George Balanchine Trust, I have the answer ready: The Trust, which licenses Balanchine ballets for performance, makes money; the Foundation spends money. This may sound flippant, but it makes a point. People do not usually ask a second time.

The Balanchine Foundation is a nonprofit corporation created in 1983, five months after Balanchine's death. (The Trust would not be founded for another four years.) Its mission is a broad one: to further the art of dance and its allied arts throughout the world, with special emphasis on the Balanchine legacy. This charge has prompted an array of programs in the areas of preservation, documentation, and education.

Balanchine said, "I am a teacher; that is my contribution." Taking this as a cue, in 1984 Barbara Horgan, president of the Foundation, made bold plans to produce a series of ten videotapes devoted to the finer points of Balanchine's ideas on classical ballet—what he taught his dancers, already thoroughly schooled in the *danse d'école,* to shape their technical abilities to his needs as a creator. (The videos most emphatically do not "teach ballet.") Horgan gave full rein to the co-authors of this ambitious undertaking: Suki Schorer, an esteemed teacher at the School of American Ballet, whom Balanchine had pegged as a teacher at an age when most dancers want nothing more than to go on dancing, and Merrill Ashley, the technically brilliant ballerina of the New York City Ballet, who had written in detail of Balanchine's teachings in her illuminating book, *Dancing for Balanchine.* (Schorer would later write an even larger volume on the subject.) The two were joined by Merrill Brockway, the award-winning television

producer and director, who had collaborated with Balanchine on five *Dance in America* programs.

Collectively known as *The Balanchine Essays,* the tapes were organized by step or group of related steps, such as "Arabesque" or "Jumps," with Schorer lecturing and Ashley demonstrating, often using choreography from well-known Balanchine ballets. Advanced students and dancers from the New York City Ballet struggled to imitate Ashley, and their "mistakes" pointed up the subtleties and complexities of Balanchine's vision. It took ten years to complete the series. Three of the programs—"Arabesque," "Attitude," and "Épaulement and Port de Bras"—are now in commercial distribution.

In 1994 I joined the Foundation in the new position of director of research. As author of a number of books on dance history and an alumna of the New York City Ballet, my bent for research and admiration for Balanchine seemed to come together in the Foundation's work. Always intrigued by process, I proposed a series of sessions on videotape in which older Balanchine dancers, on whom he created his great roles, would teach and coach these roles with dancers of today, passing on Balanchine's ideas in a uniquely direct way. The forum was particularly a propos, for Balanchine was not a verbal person about his art; he "spoke" mainly through movement and mainly in the rehearsal studio. As a writer whose trust lay in words on paper, I found my head expanding significantly to encompass the new mysteries of the world of video.

The video archive began in 1995 on an illustrious note, with Dame Alicia Markova recreating, a mere *seventy* years later, a solo from *Le Chant du Rossignol* that Balanchine had choreographed for her in 1925. They continued in high gear with Maria Tallchief on

several tapes, analyzing and coaching the dazzling *Firebird* solo and pas de deux, her signature work, as well as other ballets created around her talents from one of Balanchine's most fertile periods: *Symphony in C, Scotch Symphony, The Nutcracker, Orpheus, Sylvia Pas de Deux, Pas de Dix*, and *Allegro Brillante* (and she has yet more to show us). Frederic Franklin, premier *danseur* and *maître de ballet* of the Ballet Russe de Monte Carlo, came on board to rescue from oblivion excerpts of Balanchine ballets of the 1930s and 1940s. Interestingly, those he remembered best were those that Balanchine, like an artist painting over a canvas, rechoreographed to the same music in later years— early versions of *Le Baiser de la Fée, Raymonda,* and *Mozartiana.* Augmented by contributions from Melissa Hayden, Patricia Wilde, Todd Bolender, Rosella Hightower, Allegra Kent, Marie-Jeanne, Karin von Aroldingen, Arthur Mitchell, and Suzanne Farrell, the video archive is now composed of twenty-one master tapes (with many more awaiting editing). Copies are held in research repositories around the world.

During this collaboration, Franklin exposed his fertile mind and wealth of stories: his English birth notwithstanding, he is a living encyclopedia of ballet in America in the pioneering days of the 1930s, the 1940s, and beyond. There was nothing for it but to capture as many of his memories as possible, and the Foundation, with critic Mindy Aloff as interviewer, in association with the Jerome Robbins Dance Division of the New York Public Library for the Performing Arts, now has some sixty hours of his witty, penetrating, and insightful reminiscences safely stored on audiotape.

Another noted critic, Nancy Goldner, offered to provide tailor-made lectures to the audiences of companies presenting Balanchine programs, which, sponsored by the Foundation and the Trust, she did with great success over several years. Later she teamed with Merrill Ashley to present nationwide a related Foundation-Trust program, "Dancing Balanchine/ Watching Balanchine."

By 1999 the Foundation had a new president, Paul Epstein, self-styled "architect" of The Balanchine Trust, who had also brought the Foundation into being in 1983. (Horgan then became chairman.) An attorney with several clients in show business, Epstein had a love of musical theater that translated itself into a project known as Popular Balanchine. Its express purpose was to collect all possible information about Balanchine's commercial work—in revues, Broadway shows, operettas, and film (and not forgetting the

Maria Tallchief rehearses Judith Fugate in Sylvia Pas de Deux

circus!). Claude Conyers, emeritus vice-president and editorial director of the Scholarly and Professional Reference Department of Oxford University Press and publisher of the unprecedented and invaluable six-volume *International Encyclopedia of Dance,* was engaged to harness the efforts of more than twenty dance scholars and organize the mass of material they uncovered, which, owing to academic attitudes about the lesser importance of popular culture, had barely ever been taken seriously. A major initiative of the project was locating and interviewing those who were present at the scene—performers, creators, backstage personnel, audience members, relatives, and even fans. "Interviewing" was understood to include cajoling these durable survivors to dust off their scrapbooks and personal photos. Balanchine had only recently arrived in America when he started choreographing for Broadway and Hollywood; a major theme running through the researchers' discoveries was the extent to which his commercial work foreshadowed his later balletic masterpieces.

Epstein was also concerned with dance education at the university level and conceived an Internet-based system, Media Text, to make the materials, especially the visual materials, of dance history and performance available to students on their PCs. Software associated with the program would also give them the ability to marshall this information to support term papers and class presentations. While the costs of development are beyond the Foundation's means—and the problems with rights clearances remain seemingly insurmountable—a prototype is underway, and Epstein, whose specialty is intellectual property, may well be able to devise and engineer conditions under which copyrighted and union-restricted properties can be offered to the public over the Internet. This would be a contribution in itself.

Balanchine was praised above all else for his musicality, and a recent Foundation project, Musical Balanchine, seeks to analyze the essence of his

response to music in scholarly terms. The initial video, *Music Dances: Balanchine Choreographs Stravinsky,* by British dance and music historian Stephanie Jordan, is devoted to the seminal collaboration of two giants of twentieth-century art, with dancers of the New York City Ballet demonstrating choreographic excerpts to show the variety of ways in which Balanchine treated Stravinsky's music over the years. The issues are technical, not aesthetic. The tape does not provide an "appreciation" of *Agon,* for example, but rather cites instances of Balanchine's dance translations of pitch changes, counterpoint, polyrhythm, and atonality, among other musical devices.

As for the future, the richness of Balanchine will provide the Foundation with the impetus for many programs in years to come, and Balanchine as a subject may well be just the beginning. Many of the projects now underway are open-ended—the video archive, for example, will come to life wherever a willing Balanchine veteran (and a video camera) can be brought together. Musical Balanchine is in its early stages. Since Balanchine ballets are licensed for performance throughout the nation (and the world), the lecture series will always be relevant. Awaiting execution is the awesome task of updating and Web-mounting the 1984 catalogue of Balanchine's oeuvre— the first and still the only catalogue raisonné devoted to the output of a choreographer. I will be directing the research team.

For this dance-book author and student of Balanchine's art, what a ride it has been!

Nancy Reynolds, a former member of the New York City Ballet, has been director of research for The George Balanchine Foundation since 1994. Her books include Repertory in Review: 40 Years of the New York City Ballet, The Dance Catalog, In Performance, *and, with Malcolm McCormick,* No Fixed Points: Dance in the Twentieth Century.

Maria Tallchief and Frederic Franklin reconstructing Balanchine's first version of Baiser de la Fée

Barbara Horgan helped found The George Balanchine Trust in 1987

The George Balanchine Trust

by Lynn Garafola

Since The George Balanchine Trust was founded, it has become a model for preserving a body of choreographic work and keeping it in repertory. Copyright has a checkered history in dance, and ownership of a ballet or dance work has not always or necessarily been attributed to the choreographer. In the last third of the nineteenth century, Luigi Manzotti was able to claim ownership of ballets such as *Excelsior* in part because of the notations mapping the complicated figures and the movement of large groups of dancers that were among the attractions of spectacle ballet.[1] Petipa had no compunction about reviving—and substantially revising—ballets choreographed by others, and insisted on receiving credit for his interpolations.[2] However, the works themselves belonged to the Imperial Theaters. This was the entity that had commissioned them, paid for the music, costumes, and sets, provided the dancers to perform them and the personnel to rehearse them. Presumably, on those few occasions when a Petipa ballet (such as *The Sleeping Beauty*) was produced by a foreign company such as La Scala (which actually happened in 1896), the project required the approval of the directorate of the Imperial Theaters and, at the least, Petipa's cooperation in providing *répétiteurs* and possibly dancers. (The Scala *Beauty* was staged by Giorgio Saracco with Carlotta Brianza recreating her original role as Aurora.)[3]

In the early twentieth century, Serge Diaghilev transferred the Imperial system, with certain modifications, to his Ballets Russes. The ballets as a whole were owned by the company, which commissioned and staged them, and decided when to program them. Royalties were paid to the composer of a ballet as well as to the "author," meaning the scenarist whose name appeared on the copyright registration. This "author" was only sometimes the choreographer. It might have been the composer, as in the case of Balanchine's first collaboration with Stravinsky, *Apollon Musagète,* or a visual artist, or a writer. The poet Boris Kochno, for example, contributed the "book" to *Prodigal Son* and many other Balanchine works of the late 1920s and early 1930s. Diaghilev's choreographers smarted at what they perceived as the injustice of a system that placed choreographic originality for the first time at a premium but failed to provide adequate compensation. The Ballets Russes was both a choreographer's showcase and a showcase for new choreography, yet it was the choreographer who received short shrift.

Matters came to a head in 1937–1938, when choreographer Léonide Massine broke away from the Colonel de Basil Ballets Russes to form the rival Ballet Russe de Monte Carlo. Massine had choreographed a score of works for de Basil's company. Now he wanted to remount them on his

Maxime Belotserkovsky and Irina Dvorovenko of American Ballet Theatre in Sylvia Pas de Deux

for copyright. As intellectual property, they now had potential value. They could be passed on or inherited, like a house or a bank account or the rights to an opera or work of fiction.

Balanchine was unusually generous with his ballets. He thought of them as learning experiences for the new companies springing up around the country in the 1960s and 1970s, and consequently he often waived royalties and a fee. In the George Balanchine Archive at the Harvard Theatre Collection are hundreds of letters between the choreographer's assistant, Barbara Horgan, and companies all over the United States (as well as Europe), attesting to his generosity and the widespread dissemination of his

Mr. Balanchine with Barbara Horgan, General Director of the George Balanchine Trust

new company and demanded exclusive rights. De Basil balked: these ballets were his livelihood. The case was tried in London's Chancery Court in 1937. Massine lost. "It would be strange," Justice Luxmoore ruled, "if Colonel de Basil, having paid for the supply of that necessary ingredient [choreography] for his ballet, was himself prevented from using it."[4] In other words, Massine's choreography was work-for-hire, and as such belonged to the company that had commissioned it.

The Copyright Act of 1976 significantly revised the law governing intellectual property in the United States. Among the changes was that a

work of "choreographic expression" could now be registered by submitting a film or videotape. Before this, some kind of written material had been needed to register a dance. Traditionally, this material was either a detailed description of the story—a problem if the dance were plotless—or a detailed score in an expensive and time-consuming system such as Labanotation. (Labanotated scores, in fact, were used to register some Balanchine ballets, including *Symphony in C* and *Apollo*.) The new law meant that for the first time an inexpensive means existed to register all works of choreographic expression. In the years that followed passage of the 1976 law, the vast majority of Balanchine's works were registered

Francia Russell, Director of Pacific Northwest Ballet, rehearses her company in La Valse

ballets this helped to produce. Although Balanchine could seem diffident about the survival of his work, his actions belied this, insofar as they made his ballets part of a new national repertory crystallizing within the regional ballet movement.

Balanchine died in 1983. He left what Horgan once described as a "deficit estate with 110 ballets that in theory had value."[5] These ballets he had bequeathed to friends and colleagues. A majority went to three principal legatees: Tanaquil Le Clercq, for whom he was anxious to provide; Karin von Aroldingen, a confidante of his later years; and Horgan, his devoted assistant of decades. Additionally, there were many special bequests. To Lincoln Kirstein, the patron extraordinaire who had brought him to America a half-century earlier, Balanchine left *Concerto Barocco* and *Orpheus*, masterpieces from key moments of their shared artistic quest. A number of ballets went to the dancers who had inspired them: *Don Quixote* to Suzanne Farrell; *A Midsummer Night's Dream* to Diana Adams; *Ballo della Regina* to Merrill Ashley; *Tarantella* to Patricia McBride, *Duo Concertant* to Kay Mazzo.[6] His bequests testified to the state of his heart. They also registered a change in the relationship between a choreographer's body of work and the company that created it. Whereas Petipa's ballets belonged to the Imperial Ballet after his death, Balanchine's belonged to his heirs.

In 1987, the estate was finally settled. Horgan and von Aroldingen then formed The George Balanchine Trust, into which they deposited the rights to the ballets they owned. At the same time they invited the other legatees to join them. The result was a "centralized entity [that] could facilitate the licensing of the ballets, foster their dissemination throughout the world, and make sure that performances would be authentic and of satisfactory quality."[8] The Trust, in other words, licenses on behalf of the heirs. As Horgan explains:

Olga Chenchikova of the Kirov Ballet rehearses Sofia Gumerova in Diamonds

"During their lifetime the heirs own the rights, control the rights, get the income, and at their death they could designate the income for twenty years to as many heirs as they wanted. But the rights would stay in the trust. After twenty years the trust would continue to negotiate these rights, but at a certain point those rights would end, and they would be transferred to The George Balanchine Foundation.... So at some point in the next twenty to twenty-five years, the Foundation will become the licensor and owner of the Balanchine repertory."[9]

If a company wants to dance a Balanchine ballet, it goes to the Trust and makes the request. The Trust determines if the company is able to handle a particular work, if it has the dancers to perform it, and if it has the wherewithal to produce it and also to pay for live music. Although the Trust realizes that many companies have had to cut back on orchestras, it discourages the use of recorded music, just as it draws the line at sets and costumes that stray too far from the original.[10]

Balanchine's spirit presides over the Trust. In keeping with his generosity, it licenses ballets without charge to all kinds of educational institutions, including colleges and universities, and keeps fees appropriate to the companies that ask to license a ballet. Ballets disappear if they are not danced, and more companies are dancing Balanchine ballets today than in 1983, the year the choreographer died.[11] This is a tribute to the Trust and to its belief that dancers, companies, and audiences should have access to Balanchine's choreography.

The real heroes of the Trust story are the "*répétiteurs*," the former New York City Ballet dancers who stage Balanchine's works on behalf of the Trust and give the "seal of approval," so to speak, to works in repertory. The *répétiteurs*, representing several generations of Balanchine dancers, include Francia Russell and Victoria Simon, dancers who joined NYCB in the 1950s and staged their first ballets in the 1960s and 1970s. There are former

The Pennsylvania Ballet in The Nutcracker

Pacific Northwest Ballet in Agon

ballerinas like Suzanne Farrell and Karin von Aroldingen (who is also one of the Trust's dancer-trustees), distinguished teachers such as Suki Schorer and Susan Pilarre, mavericks such as Patricia Neary, who work largely in Europe, and many others. Along with the older group of *répétiteurs* who worked closely with Balanchine is a younger group that knows him chiefly—or even solely—through his ballets.

Balanchine lived in the present. "I can see no need for preservation," he once said."A ballet is a movement in time and space, a living moment. Like a hothouse flower, it blooms, then dies."[12] Thanks to The George Balanchine Trust his work will defy—at least for a time—the oblivion into which even the most celebrated ballets of the past have vanished. For this we must all be grateful. ✤

Lynn Garafola is a critic and historian living in New York City. She is the author of Diaghilev's Ballets Russes and was curator of the exhibition "Dance for a City: Fifty Years of the New York City Ballet." She teaches at Barnard College.

Makharbek Vaziev, Director of the Kirov Ballet, and Karin von Aroldingen rehearse the Kirov Ballet in Diamonds

---

NOTES

1. For a fascinating discussion of copyright and ownership in this era in Europe, see Concetta Lo Iacono, "Manzotti e Marenco: Il diritto di due autori," *Nuova Rivista Musicale Italiana*, vol. 21, no. 3 (July–Sept. 1987), pp. 421–446.

2. See, for example, his letter to Alexei Suvorin, publisher of the St. Petersburg newspaper *Novoe Vremia* (New Times), in which he insisted on his authorship of the children's mazurka and a "new grand pas" in the last act of *Paquita*, first choreographed by Joseph Mazilier in 1846. Quoted in Lynn Garafola, "Introduction," *The Diaries of Marius Petipa, Studies in Dance History*, vol. 3, no. 1 (Spring 1992), p. xiii.

3. For this 1896 revival, see George Jackson and Peter Gogel, "The Italian 'Beauty' of 1896: First Full Production in the West," *Ballet Review*, vol. 2, no. 6 (1969), pp. 24–27.

4. Quoted in Jack Anderson, *The One and Only: The Ballet Russe de Monte Carlo* (New York: Dance Horizons, 1981), p. 7.

5. "A Conversation with Barbara Horgan," conducted by Lynn Garafola at Barnard College on October 8, 2001, as part of the "On Dance" series of public programs sponsored by the Department of Dance.

6. Bernard Taper, *Balanchine: A Biography*, rev. ed. (Berkeley: University of California Press, 1996), p. 401.

7. Ibid., p. 402.

8. Ibid., p. 404.

9. "A Conversation with Barbara Horgan."

10. Ibid.

11. Ibid.

12. *By George Balanchine* (New York: San Marco Press, 1984), p. 11.

New York City Ballet in Rubies

Index